READER BONUS!

Dear Reader,

As a thank you for your support, Action Takers Publishing would like to offer you a special reader bonus: a free download of our course, "How to Write, Publish, Market & Monetize Your Book the Fast, Fun & Easy Way." This comprehensive course is designed to provide you with the tools and knowledge you need to bring your book to life and turn it into a successful venture.

The course typically **retails for $499**, but as a valued reader, you can access it for free. To claim your free download, simply follow this link ActionTakersPublishing.com/workshops - use the discount code "coursefree" to get a 100% discount and start writing your book today.

If we are still giving away this course by the time you're reading this book, head straight over to your computer and start the course now. It's absolutely free.

READER BONUS!

ActionTakersPublishing.com/workshops
discount code "coursefree"

UNSTOPPABLE

FEMALE ENTREPRENEURS
LIVING FEARLESSLY

© Copyright Action Takers Publishing Inc 2024

All rights reserved. No part of this publication may be reproduced or transmitted in any form or by any means, mechanical or electronic, including photocopying and recording, or by any information storage and retrieval system, without permission in writing from publisher (except by reviewer, who may quote brief sections and/or show brief video clips in a review).

Disclaimer: The Publisher makes no representations or warranties with respect to the accuracy or completeness of the contents of this work and specifically disclaims all warranties, including without limitation warranties of fitness for a particular purpose. No warranty may be created or suitable for every situation. This works is sold with the understanding that the Publisher is not engaged in rendering legal, accounting, or other professional services. If professional assistance is required, the services of a competent professional person should be sought.

Neither the Publisher nor the Authors shall be liable for damages arising herefrom. The fact that an organization or website is referred to in this work as a referred source of further information does not mean that the Author or the Publisher endorse the information the organization or website may provide or recommendations it may make. Further, readers should be aware that websites listed in this work may have changed or disappeared between when this work was written and when it was read.

Email: lynda@actiontakerspublishing.com

Website: www.actiontakerspublishing.com

ISBN # (paperback) 978-1-956665-48-2

ISBN # (Kindle) 978-1-956665-49-9

Published by Action Takers Publishing™

Table of Contents

Introduction 1

Chapter 1: Embracing the Unstoppable Journey of Fearless Transformation
by Lynda Sunshine West 5

Chapter 2: The Journey of a Resilient Entrepreneur
by Sally Larkin Green 27

Chapter 3: Life After Fear, My Unstoppable Journey
by Adele Rose 45

Chapter 4: The Four Words That Changed My Life
by Alice Dartnell 59

Chapter 5: Seasoned Strategies for Entrepreneurial Success
by Diana L. Howles 77

Chapter 6: Replace the Old Burden With the New Version of You
by Fari Eskandari Gonzaque 93

Chapter 7: Say Yes to the Opportunity
by Jacalyn M. Price 109

TABLE OF CONTENTS

Chapter 8: From Setbacks to Success: Lessons in Entrepreneurship and Resilience
by Julie Page 127

Chapter 9: Mission First, People Always
by Kathi Sohn 145

Chapter 10: Pegasus, Like a Phoenix Rising
by Mary-Frances Buckland 157

Chapter 11: Faith, Self-Worth, and Confidence
by S. Kay McBreairty 171

Chapter 12: Finding My Roots: A Journey of Entrepreneurship
by Sophie Teixeira de Abreu 187

Chapter 13: When Nothing Is What It Seems
by Sylvia Chavez 203

Introduction

In a world where challenges abound, where barriers rise as fast as dreams take flight, there exists a breed of individuals who refuse to be bound by limitations. They are the fearless female entrepreneurs, the modern-day warriors of ambition and innovation. They are the embodiment of determination, resilience, and unwavering belief in themselves and their visions.

"Unstoppable: Female Entrepreneurs Living Fearlessly" is a celebration of these remarkable women, the driving force behind their businesses, and the architects of their destinies. Within these pages, we journey into the hearts and minds of these dynamic individuals who have shattered glass ceilings, toppled obstacles, and carved paths to success where none existed before.

Their stories are as diverse as the industries they have conquered, yet they share a common thread – an

INTRODUCTION

unyielding spirit that refuses to accept defeat. Through trials and tribulations, they've emerged not only as business leaders but as advocates for change, mentors, and inspirations to countless others.

Let's embark on this unforgettable journey, guided by these fearless authors and their chapters:

1. Embracing the Unstoppable Journey of Fearless Transformation by Lynda Sunshine West
2. The Journey of a Resilient Entrepreneur by Sally Larkin Green
3. Life After Fear, My Unstoppable Journey by Adele Rose
4. The Four Words That Changed My Life by Alice Dartnell
5. Seasoned Strategies for Entrepreneurial Success by Diana L. Howles
6. Replace the Old Burden With the New Version of You by Fari Eskandari Gonzaque
7. Say Yes to the Opportunity by Jacalyn M. Price
8. From Setbacks to Success: Lessons in Entrepreneurship and Resilience by Julie Page
9. Mission First, People Always by Kathi Sohn

10. Pegasus, Like a Phoenix Rising by Mary-Frances Buckland
11. Faith, Self-Worth, and Confidence by S. Kay McBreairty
12. Finding My Roots: A Journey of Entrepreneurship by Sophie Teixeira de Abreu
13. When Nothing Is What It Seems by Sylvia Chavez

In "Unstoppable," you'll find the experiences, lessons, and insights of these fearless authors who have dared to dream big and worked tirelessly to make those dreams a reality. They divulge their strategies for overcoming imposter syndrome, finding self-love, and harnessing personal development to achieve greatness. They demonstrate how they've turned adversity and challenges into their greatest gifts and discovered the true meaning of freedom, joy, celebration, hope, and belief.

"Unstoppable" is more than just a collection of stories; it's a testament to the power of determination, the resilience of the human spirit, and the limitless potential that resides within each of us. It's a guidebook for those who aspire to greatness, a source of inspiration for those facing obstacles, and a reminder that, indeed, nothing is impossible for the fearless female entrepreneur.

So, turn the page, embrace the journey, and let the tales of these unstoppable women inspire you to live fearlessly and chase your own dreams with unwavering resolve.

CHAPTER 1

Embracing the Unstoppable Journey of Fearless Transformation

by Lynda Sunshine West

At age 51, I found myself at a significant turning point. After a dizzying array of jobs – 49 in just three years – including my last role working for a judge in the Ninth Circuit Court of Appeals, I took a deep breath and stepped into the world of entrepreneurship. This wasn't a calculated, well-planned move. It was a leap driven by a burning passion to help others, even though I had no concrete plan or clear idea of how to make a living from this newfound path. It was a leap into a dream fueled by the desire to make an impact, to transform lives, and in doing so, to rediscover myself.

I was driving to work one day, my 49th job, when I suddenly had an epiphany moment. You know, that moment where the world stops spinning and time stands still so you can take it all in and become open to new opportunities and new possibilities. I had the realization that I hated my life (well, most of my life). I felt like a caged animal that was let out every day for "exercise" to work for people I didn't like working for doing work that I hated doing. The worst part? I built that cage for myself. As I worked my way up the corporate ladder, I was achieving what I wanted, success.

That epiphany led to me making the smartest move of my entire life. I hired a life coach who helped me discover who I am, what value I have to offer this world, and my next step: quit my job and become an entrepreneur.

That led to the next smartest move my greatest challenge: breaking through one fear every day for an entire year. I was 51 years old and realized you're never too old to start something new.

A Childhood Marked by Adventure and Fear

My relationship with fear began earlier than most. At the tender age of five, I embarked on an unexpected adventure, running away from home… for a week. The week-long escapade, while short, cast a long shadow over my childhood, leaving me with a deep-seated sense of fear and uncertainty. Don't worry. I was safe. I was just at the neighbor's house and was safe. My mom knew where I was, but I didn't know she knew where I was. This is an important piece of my story because that one week created within me a belief I would carry around with me the next 46 years, the belief that no one came to get me because they didn't love me and didn't want me around. I returned home changed, carrying with me the seeds of fears that would grow silently within me, shaping my future in ways I couldn't yet comprehend.

Navigating Life as a People-Pleaser

My early experiences with fear led me down a path of people-pleasing. It became my mechanism for coping with the world – always smiling, always agreeable, perpetually seeking validation and acceptance from those around me. This approach to life was my shield, protecting me from confrontation and the judgment of others, but at the cost of losing my own voice and identity. I didn't know who I was and didn't know I didn't know. It was not until my pivot to entrepreneurship at age 51 that I began to confront my deep-rooted fears, setting the stage for a year of remarkable transformation. As a people-pleaser, it was impossible to know who I was. I spent my waking hours doing for others so they would like me. By the time I figured this out, I was about 54 years old. I'm just glad I did.

The Decision to Embrace Courage

The day I decided to confront a fear every day for an entire year was not marked by any grand event or external push; it was a quiet resolve born from a place of deep introspection. Having spent decades in a self-constructed cage of people-pleasing and unfulfilling jobs, I realized I had been merely existing, not truly living. At 51, I stood on the precipice of a life-changing realization: to live fully, I needed to face the very things that scared me the most.

That decision was more than a challenge; it was a commitment to myself. It was about reclaiming my life, piece by piece, fear by fear. I wanted to prove to myself, and perhaps to the world, that age is just a number and it's never too late to reinvent yourself. 2015 was to be my battleground, where I would confront the ghosts of fears past and the uncertainties of the future.

While it was scary, it was the greatest experience ever. The growth that transpired was like nothing I expected. I didn't even know it was possible to transform that much in such a short period of time. What made my transformation so fast? I was completely open to learning and growing and didn't allow my negative beliefs about myself to stop me from moving forward. I embraced the changes with open arms and challenged myself daily to break through fears and love every minute of it.

Motivations Rooted in Transformation

The underlying motivation for this daring undertaking stemmed from a profound desire for transformation. I was tired of being a spectator in my own life, watching days turn into years without a sense of fulfillment or purpose. I remember banging my hands on the steering wheel of my car while I was stuck in traffic and yelling at the top of my lungs, "I have no value. I have no purpose. I have no reason for being here. Why am I on this planet? As a matter of fact, why is this planet here?" I yearned to break free from the chains of fear that had restricted my potential and to discover who I truly was beneath the layers of societal expectations and self-imposed limitations. I wanted to know my purpose, if I even had a purpose.

Each day's challenge was a step towards liberation – from fears, from doubts, from judgment, from the shadows of my past. It was about building resilience, learning to trust my instincts, and above all, understanding that the only approval I needed was my own. This journey was not just about overcoming fear; it was about forging a path to a life that was genuinely mine, one fearless step at a time.

Embarking on the Journey

As I embarked on this journey, I was acutely aware that it would not be easy. There would be days when my resolve would falter, fears that seemed insurmountable, and moments of doubt. But the promise of growth, of evolving into a stronger, more authentic version of myself, was the beacon that guided me through. Each fear faced was a victory, each day a triumph over the old self, and with each step, I was becoming unstoppable.

Every morning… 365 days in a row… I would wake up and, before my feet hit the floor, ask myself a simple question, three words that would change my life: "What scares me?" After I asked the question, I would lay in bed and wait until the answer came. My "commitment" to myself was to break through that fear that day. I never knew what fear was going to come up and some were pretty random like "talk to a stranger in Starbucks," "go to a movie by yourself," "go to a restaurant and say 'only one in my party,'" or "go to a networking event and start a conversation," and the list goes on (for 365 days). While these may not be fears to you, they were extremely debilitating fears for me.

I came to the greatest realization in my life: the majority of my fears were based on the fear of judgment. If you look at my fears above, you'll notice a common theme, the fear of what people will think of me. Let's examine these fears to see where judgment showed up for me and it may show up for you, too. After all, the fear of judgment is the #1 fear of the majority of people.

Action to Take	**My Fear**	**The Reality**
Talk to a stranger in Starbucks	What if I say something stupid and embarrass myself?	I may say something stupid and embarrass myself, but I'll "get over it" shortly after I've left Starbucks. It's okay to embarrass myself as long as I don't let it stop me from living my life. I embarrass myself all the time now and have fun with it. I don't let it adversely affect my life.

EMBRACING THE UNSTOPPABLE JOURNEY OF FEARLESS TRANSFORMATION

Action to Take	My Fear	The Reality
Go to a movie by myself	What if people feel sorry for me because I'm all alone and talk about me behind my back?	No one is noticing me. There's nothing for me to fear. They're all wrapped up in the movie or in their own lives.
Go to a restaurant and say "only one in my party"	What if people feel sorry for me because I'm all alone and talk about me behind my back?	No one is noticing me. There's nothing for me to fear. They're all wrapped up in their food and their cell phones and don't even notice I'm there.
Go to a networking event and start a conversation	What if I stutter? What if I don't know what to say? How do I start a conversation? What will they think of me? Will I be dressed right?	Most people who go to networking are also scared and are experiencing the same fears as I am. This means that if I start a conversation, I'm helping them through their fears as well as my own. The majority of times when I've started a conversation with someone, I was glad I did because we got along and had something in common.

You see, by looking deeply into my fears, I noticed that they were mostly based on the fear of judgment. "What if people XYZ?" The fear of judgment is prevalent in most of our lives. By breaking through one fear a day for a year, I have pretty much rid myself of that fear. I decided about three months into breaking through the fears that my fear of judgment was the one fear I was going to tackle to see how I could crush it and start to really live my life. So that's exactly what I did.

Embracing Fear as a Catalyst for Growth

In my book "Do It BECAUSE You're Scared," I discuss the transformative power of embracing fear. This journey taught me that fear is not an obstacle to be avoided but a catalyst for growth and self-discovery. Each fear I faced was an opportunity to stretch beyond my comfort zone, to learn, and to evolve.

The Seven Simple Steps to Break Through Fear Every Time

Throughout my year of facing fears, I relied on a set of principles, which I later termed "The Seven Simple Steps to Break Through Fear Every Time." These steps became my roadmap, guiding me through each challenge:

EMBRACING THE UNSTOPPABLE JOURNEY OF FEARLESS TRANSFORMATION

Acknowledgment/Awareness: Recognizing and accepting the presence of fear was the first step. It's about facing the truth head-on, not hiding from it or pretending it doesn't exist.

Understanding: I sought to understand the root of my fears. Why was I scared of judgment? What past experiences were fueling this fear? This understanding was crucial for navigating through it.

Reframing: Seeing fear from a different perspective was transformative. Instead of viewing it as a barrier, I saw it as a stepping stone towards personal growth.

Commitment: Committing to face the fear was essential. This meant not just acknowledging it, but actively deciding to confront it no matter how uncomfortable it felt.

Strategizing: Developing a strategy or plan for facing each fear made the process more manageable. Whether it was talking to a stranger or attending a networking event, having a plan gave me a sense of control.

Action: The most critical step was taking action. Nothing happens without action. It's one thing to plan, but another to actually do it. Each action, no matter how small, was a victory against fear.

Reflection: After facing each fear, I reflected on the experience. What did I learn? How did it feel? This reflection helped solidify the growth and learning from each experience.

The Power of Vulnerability and Authenticity

Another key insight from my book, and one that was pivotal in my journey, was the power of vulnerability and authenticity. By being open about my fears, not only to myself but to others, I found strength. It created a space for genuine connections and taught me the value of being my true self, without the masks and facades I had worn for years. By sharing my fears with others, they saw me as brave. Here I was feeling weak because I had these fears, but others were seeing my strength for being vulnerable and sharing my fears. So I came up with this quote:

"Be brave and share your weaknesses,
for in your weaknesses others see your
strengths."
~Lynda Sunshine West

Turning Fear into Fuel

Ultimately, "Do It BECAUSE You're Scared" is about turning fear into fuel for personal and professional growth. This journey taught me that fear, when embraced and understood, can be a powerful force for positive change. We can let our fears FAIL us or FUEL us. It's our choice and is one of my favorite parts of being human. We have the power of choice. It's about moving from a place of fear to a place of empowerment, where each challenge is an opportunity to learn, grow, and become more of who you truly are.

Facing the Fear of Rejection

One of my most transformative fears was the fear of rejection. It's a fear that had silently dictated many of my life choices. To confront this, I decided to put myself in situations where rejection was a real possibility. One such instance was when I pitched an idea to a group of potential collaborators. The fear of hearing 'no' was palpable, but I went ahead. The outcome? I did face rejection, but it wasn't the end of the world. Instead, it became a lesson in resilience. I learned that rejection was not a reflection of my worth but rather a part of the journey toward success.

Overcoming the Fear of Failure

Another significant fear was the fear of failure, especially as a new entrepreneur. I took a chance on a project that was way outside my comfort zone. There was a risk of failing spectacularly, but I pushed forward. Though the project had its ups and downs, it ultimately led to unexpected success and opened doors to new opportunities. This experience taught me that failure is not the opposite of success; it's a crucial part of it. Embracing the possibility of failure allowed me to take risks that led to growth and learning.

Conquering the Fear of Being Alone

A personal fear that I tackled was the fear of being alone. This fear had led me to stay in unfulfilling situations. I challenged this by spending time alone, doing activities like solo dining and traveling. These experiences were initially daunting, but they taught me the value of my own company and the strength of independence. I discovered a newfound sense of self-reliance and confidence.

Transforming the Fear of Speaking My Truth

Perhaps the most empowering fear I faced was the fear of speaking my truth, especially in situations where my opinions differed from others. I started expressing my thoughts and beliefs more openly, whether in personal conversations or public speaking engagements. This not only strengthened my voice but also attracted people who resonated with my authenticity. It was a liberating experience that reinforced the power of being true to oneself.

Key Takeaways from a Year of Facing Fears

Takeaway #1 One of the most significant lessons I learned is the strength in vulnerability. I believe our vulnerability is our greatest strength as human beings. Acknowledging and confronting fears is not a sign of weakness, but a testament to courage. It allows for personal growth and genuine connections.

Takeaway #2 Each fear you face and overcome reinforces the idea that resilience is not about never falling but about how quickly we get back up. It's about facing challenges, learning from them, and moving forward with renewed strength.

Takeaway #3 Living authentically, speaking my truth, and being true to my values brought a sense of fulfillment that no amount of people-pleasing ever did. Learning how to be authentic attracted the right opportunities and people into my life.

Takeaway #4 Stepping out of my comfort zone was where I found the most significant growth. It was in these moments of discomfort that I discovered new abilities and untapped potential. The size of my comfort zone was enlarged exponentially and it's going to keep growing because I'm in it for the long haul. Bring on the fears. You can't stop me anymore.

Takeaway #5 Fear, I learned, is not something to be eradicated but understood and used as a guide and as fuel to help you grow. It often points us towards areas where we need to grow and can lead to incredible breakthroughs.

Application to Entrepreneurship

As a female entrepreneur, embracing vulnerability has allowed me to lead with empathy and authenticity. This approach fosters a culture of trust and openness within my team and with clients. I have developed an amount of resilience I didn't even know I possessed. It has been crucial in navigating the unpredictable waters of entrepreneurship. It's about adapting to changes, overcoming setbacks, and continually striving for improvement.

Being true to myself has helped in building a brand that resonates with my core values. Once I learned who I am, I was able to incorporate my core values into not only my personal life, but also my business life. Three weeks into breaking through my fears, I made a personal life declaration. I claimed, "I will spend the rest of my life having as much fun as possible, hanging out with positive and uplifting people who are making a positive impact on the planet." This personal declaration has created exactly what I set out for it to create. You're reading this story because YOU are my people. YOU are positive and uplifting and you're making a greater impact on the planet. Thank you for being YOU!! My authenticity attracts people who share similar values and beliefs, creating more meaningful and lasting relationships.

The willingness (which has transformed into eagerness) to step out of my comfort zone has led to innovative ideas and business strategies. It's about taking calculated risks and being open to new possibilities, even if they seem daunting at first. In business, fears can often highlight areas that require attention or development. Acknowledging and addressing these fears has been instrumental in my growth as an entrepreneur and the growth of my business.

From Fear to Book Publishing

The journey to founding Action Takers Publishing was as much a leap of faith as it was a natural progression of my transformation. By the time I had confronted my fears for a year, I had not only reshaped my own narrative but had also ignited a deep-seated passion to help others do the same. The idea for Action Takers Publishing germinated from this newfound purpose.

The transition from being a people-pleaser to an entrepreneur was filled with challenges, but each fear I faced equipped me with the resilience and confidence needed to embark on this new path. It was during a moment of reflection that I realized the power of stories. I had always believed in the transformative power of sharing experiences, and now I wanted to create a platform where others could do the same.

Action Takers Publishing was born from the desire to turn visions into reality. It wasn't just about publishing books; it was about giving voice to the unheard, about turning the whispers of dreams into loud, proud declarations. The name itself, 'Action Takers,' reflected the ethos of the company: to encourage and support those who dare to take the leap, to move from thinking to doing, from dreaming to achieving.

Empowering Others Through Storytelling

My mission with Action Takers Publishing is clear: to empower 5 million women and men to share their stories with the world to make a greater impact on the planet. This mission was deeply aligned with my own journey of self-discovery and transformation. Just as I had learned the importance of facing fears and embracing authenticity, I wanted to provide a platform for others to do the same. I found that the more I shared my story, the more I encouraged others to do the same.

Each book we publish is more than just a collection of words; it's a life, a journey, an inspiration. It's an opportunity for authors to not only share their unique stories but also to inspire, educate, and empower readers. We don't just publish books; we help create movements, spark conversations, and ignite change.

By helping authors bring their stories to life, we are contributing to a greater narrative, one of courage, resilience, and transformation. Our authors come from diverse backgrounds and experiences, yet they all share one common trait: the courage to take action and to share their truths with the world.

By enabling these voices to be heard, Action Takers Publishing is not just a publishing house; it's a beacon of hope, a testament to the power of overcoming fears and embracing one's true self. It's about making a greater impact on the planet, one story at a time.

Reflecting on Being Unstoppable

My journey, from facing a fear every day to founding Action Takers Publishing, has profoundly reshaped my understanding of what it means to be unstoppable. To be unstoppable is not about never experiencing fear; it's about moving forward BECAUSE you're scared. It's about turning vulnerabilities into strengths and challenges into opportunities.

Being unstoppable means embracing change, not just as an inevitable part of life, but as a powerful force for growth and transformation. It's about realizing that the only limits that truly exist are the ones we place on ourselves. Through my journey, I discovered that being unstoppable is less about what you achieve and more about the journey of transformation — the process of continually evolving, learning, and pushing beyond perceived boundaries.

To you, the reader, standing at the precipice of your own journey, I extend a heartfelt invitation. Embark on your own path of facing fears. It doesn't have to be as drastic as facing a fear every day for a year; it just needs to be a commitment to step out of and enlarge the size of your comfort zone, to challenge the fears that hold you back.

Start with one fear, one step. Ask yourself, "What you I do if I weren't afraid?" Then go do that. Make a commitment to yourself to transform your life into who you are here meant to be and be that person. Let the, "What scares me?" guide you towards actions that may seem small but are significant in breaking the chains of fear. Remember, every giant leap begins with a small, uncertain step.

Use your fears as signposts pointing you toward growth and self-discovery. Embrace them, understand them, and use them as fuel to propel you forward. Your fears are not your enemy; they are your teachers, your allies, on the journey to becoming who you are meant to be.

And most importantly, know that you are not alone. We are all on this journey together, each of us learning, stumbling, and rising in our own ways. Share your stories, your fears, your victories. In doing so, you not only empower yourself but also inspire others to do the same.

So, take that step, face that fear, embrace your journey, and become the unstoppable force you are destined to be. The world is waiting for your story.

"Faith Erases Anxious Reactions."
~Lynda Sunshine West

Lynda Sunshine West

She ran away at 5 years old and was gone an entire week, came home riddled with fears and, in turn, became a people-pleaser. At age 51, she decided to break through one fear every day for a year and, in doing so, she gained an exorbitant amount of confidence to share her story. Her mission is to empower 5 million women and men to write their stories to make a greater impact on the planet.

Lynda Sunshine West is the Founder and CEO of Action Takers Publishing, a Bestseller Book Publishing Expert, Speaker, 38 Time #1 International Bestselling Author, Contributing Writer at Entrepreneur Magazine, Senior Level Executive Contributing Writer at Brainz

Magazine, Executive Film Producer, and Red Carpet Celebrity Interviewer.

Connect with Lynda Sunshine at

https://www.ActionTakersPublishing.com.

CHAPTER 2

The Journey of a Resilient Entrepreneur

by Sally Larkin Green

*I dedicate this to all the women in my life
who have loved and supported me.*

Every woman has a story. But what if her story isn't just about the path she walked, but the challenges she overcame? Imagine a journey marked not just by the steps forward but by the resilience shown in the face of daunting challenges. This is the story of the unstoppable female entrepreneur - a story of rising above adversity, of stepping outside comfort zones despite deep-seated fears and doubts. This is my story about learning resilience, not by choice, but by necessity.

How do we ignite this indomitable spirit in our businesses and transform our dreams into enduring legacies? It is a journey of understanding the essence of standing tall amidst adversity, carving new paths where none exist, and embodying the spirit of the unstoppable.

Another critical aspect of resilience is self-love and self-care. In a society where women are often expected to put others first, prioritizing oneself can be a radical act. However, it is essential. Embracing self-love and becoming a self-care rockstar is not just about indulgence; it's about recognizing that to be effective in our roles - as entrepreneurs, mothers, and wives - we need to be physically, emotionally, and mentally at our best.

I'll never forget the morning I woke up, looked in the mirror, and thought; "Wow, I'm a total mess!" Emotionally, mentally, spiritually, financially, physically – you name it, I was at rock bottom. It hit me that I needed to switch things up big time. See, I was really good at taking care of everything – my family, my pets, my business – but when it came to taking care of myself, I was a total failure.

Right then and there, I decided it was time for some serious self-care and self-love, something I hadn't done in a long time. I started eating better and exercising. I started reading self-help books for the first time in ages. I turned off the TV and enrolled in online courses. Then I received an amazing opportunity to be part of a multi-author book. Joining that book was a game-changer for me. It spurred growth in me like never before.

Looking back, I barely recognize the woman I was 4-5 years ago. It has been a complete transformation, and I'm so glad I started taking better care of myself.

Picture yourself completely swamped, juggling your business, marriage, motherhood, and household responsibilities. You're going through the motions, yet inside, there's a feeling of being underappreciated and overwhelmed. Your daily tasks feel like they are on repeat, and your desire to push forward wanes. This is a point of stagnation, marked by depression and a lack of clear direction. What, then, is resilience in such times?

Resilience is being strong enough to bend but not break under pressure. It's about looking beyond the immediate challenges to see positive outcomes, and holding steadfast to your dreams even when circumstances seem bleak. It involves sharing your doubts and fears in the face of adversity and believing in a brighter, better future.

Throughout my life, there have been moments of overwhelming pressure where quitting seemed like the only option - and, admittedly, there were times I succumbed to that urge. However, learning to stick it out and becoming unstoppable wasn't an inherent trait but a skill I cultivated over time. There were instances where I persevered in jobs and situations that seemed insurmountable, but it was through these experiences that I discovered my true strength.

Adversity, while daunting, is a powerful teacher. It strips away the non-essentials, focusing our energies on what truly matters. For a female entrepreneur, adversity is not just an obstacle; it's an opportunity to demonstrate strength, innovation, and growth. It is in these moments that we find our true capabilities, pushing beyond the limits we once thought were unbreakable.

In 2020, I did something pretty cool – I raised my hand to be part of this amazing collaboration book. Imagine being part of a book with 150 successful business owners, actors, actresses, and coaches. And then there's me, feeling a bit like the new kid on the block. But then I had this lightbulb moment: I asked myself, "How could I leverage this opportunity?"

Here's what I did. I hopped on Facebook and reached out to every author in that book. I sent them personal messages, introducing myself and letting them know I was excited to be part of the same book project. I asked about what they were up to and how I could support them. A bunch of them accepted my friend requests, and we started a conversation and became friends. Not everyone got back to me, but that's part of the game. But it was through those who did, that I managed to shift my perspective, really find direction, and get a clear sense of what I wanted and where I was headed in life.

One key element in overcoming adversity is a support network. In my journey, reaching out and building relationships with other authors in the anthology books I have been part of has been transformational. It has opened doors to opportunities and fostered friendships that were instrumental in my growth. These connections provided not just professional benefits but also personal ones. The emotional support I have received has been crucial in navigating my entrepreneurial journey.

Then I embarked on an exciting yet daunting venture: starting a YouTube show. Despite having zero followers and minimal experience, I was thrilled when three incredible individuals agreed to be interviewed on my show. But self-doubt crept in. One morning, filled with uncertainty, I impulsively deleted the website I had been working on and decided to cancel the show and the interviews before they had even happened. I was convinced no one would be interested in what I had to say or in being interviewed by an unknown like me. This was a pattern for me, backing away just when things were about to take off. But this time, I chose differently. I recreated the website and kept the interviews. That decision marked a turning point for me. It was a crucial part of my journey, a lesson in embracing the power of an Unstoppable Attitude and not quitting when filled with doubt.

One thing that has stuck with me is this advice: Always keep your cup filled to overflowing, and only give to others from the overflow. When I heard that, it clicked. For years, I'd been giving to others and draining myself dry, barely refilling my cup. But learning how to keep my cup overflowing has been my secret sauce these last few years. Taking care of me first isn't selfish; it's essential.

As we forge ahead, it's crucial to keep sight of the bigger picture. Our journey as female entrepreneurs isn't just about personal success; it's about paving the way for others. It's about creating a legacy of strong, resilient, and unstoppable women who believe in their dreams and dare to pursue them, despite the odds and despite the setbacks. I have learned a few Life Lessons on this journey I would like to share.

Life Lesson 1: Embrace Failure as a Steppingstone

One of the most vital lessons on the path to becoming an unstoppable entrepreneur is learning to view failure not as a setback but as a steppingstone. Failure, often feared and avoided, is a rich source of learning and growth. In my journey, I have faced numerous failures - projects that didn't take off, ideas that were met with skepticism, and times when I doubted my capabilities. However, each failure brought with it valuable lessons. It taught me about what doesn't work, pushing me to innovate and try new approaches. Failure, in essence, became a classroom where I learned some of my most crucial lessons in resilience.

Embracing failure requires a shift in perspective. It involves understanding that every failed attempt is a part of the larger process of succeeding. It's about dissecting these experiences to glean insights and strategies for the future. This approach transforms the daunting image of failure into a necessary step towards success.

Life Lesson 2: Build a Resilient Mindset - Crafting Your Toolkit

Resilience isn't just something you're born with; it's a skill cultivated with intention and care. Over my years as a mentor, author, and entrepreneur, I've meticulously crafted what I fondly refer to as my 'resilience toolkit.' This collection of practices and mindsets isn't just a strategy; it's a lifeline that keeps me anchored in the tumultuous sea of life's challenges.

A cornerstone of my toolkit is mindfulness, a practice that nurtures a calm, yet focused, state of mind, even amidst the most chaotic circumstances. This mindfulness isn't passive; it's an active engagement with the present, a way to center myself and make decisions from a place of clarity.

Equally powerful is the art of positive self-talk. We all have that inner critic, especially during tough times, but I've learned to counter it with affirmations of strength and capability. This positive self-dialogue is not just wishful thinking; it's a strategic tool in reshaping my mindset to one of resilience and perseverance.

Celebrating small victories is another key component. In the fast-paced world of publishing and mentoring, it's easy to overlook the smaller milestones. Yet, it's these moments that are the steppingstones to larger successes. Each small win is a testament to progress, a reminder that every effort, no matter how minor it seems, is moving me closer to my ultimate goals.

Now, let's talk about the three additional elements you've added to your toolkit: Morning and evening visualization, a written set of goals, and unwavering faith in God with the belief that 'this too shall pass.'

1. **Morning and Evening Visualization**: This is a powerful technique where I start and end my day with a clear mental image of my aspirations and the person I strive to be. It's like setting the stage in the morning and then reviewing the play in the evening. This consistent visualization reinforces my goals and keeps me aligned with my purpose.

2. **A Written Set of Goals**: There's something almost magical about putting pen to paper. My written goals are not just reminders; they are commitments I make to myself. They serve as a roadmap, guiding me through the daily hustle and keeping me focused on the bigger picture. This list is dynamic, evolving as I grow and achieve.

3. **Unwavering Faith in God:** My faith is the bedrock of my resilience. In moments of doubt or hardship, it's my faith that whispers, 'This too shall pass.' It's a deep-seated belief that there's a higher plan and that every challenge is an opportunity to grow and learn. This faith doesn't make problems disappear, but it gives me the strength to face them head-on.

This resilience toolkit isn't just a set of practices; it's a way of life. It's about transforming challenges into opportunities for growth, staying grounded in the face of adversity, and moving steadily toward the life I envision. Whether it's through mindfulness, positive self-talk, celebrating small victories, visualization, goal setting, or faith, each tool plays a crucial role in building a resilient and fulfilling life.

Life Lesson 3: Cultivate a Network of Support and Mentorship

In the dynamic and often unpredictable journey of entrepreneurship, having a support network isn't just beneficial; it's essential. This network, composed of mentors, peers, and colleagues, forms a foundational pillar for not only professional growth but personal resilience as well.

A support network is more than a collection of contacts; it's a web of relationships that offer diverse perspectives, wisdom, and encouragement. In my journey, this network has been a lifeline during times of uncertainty and a sounding board for new ideas. Whether it's navigating the complexities of the publishing world or managing my health, the collective experience and knowledge within my network have often illuminated the path forward.

Key Benefits of building a network of unstoppable colleagues and mentors:

1. **Guidance and Insight:** Each member of your network brings unique experiences and expertise. This diversity of thought is invaluable in offering fresh perspectives and innovative solutions to challenges.

2. **Emotional Support and Encouragement:** Entrepreneurship can be a lonely path. Having a network means there are people who understand your struggles and can offer empathy and motivation.

3. **Opportunities for Collaboration and Growth:** Through your network, doors open to new collaborations, partnerships, and opportunities that might otherwise remain inaccessible.

Mentorship is a key component of this network, a mutually enriching relationship. As a mentee, learning from seasoned professionals offers a shortcut to wisdom, helping to avoid common pitfalls and accelerate growth. These mentors, with their wealth of experience, provide not just tactical advice but also strategic insights that shape decision-making processes.

Being a mentor brings its own set of rewards. It's an opportunity to give back, to share the lessons learned on your journey. But it's more than just teaching; it's about learning too. Engaging with mentees exposes me to new ideas, fresh perspectives, and innovative approaches. It keeps me connected to the evolving landscape of my field, ensuring that my knowledge and skills remain sharp and relevant.

Engaging in mentorship and building supportive networks is, at its core, an act of service. By investing time and energy in others, we not only contribute to their growth but also to the broader community. This service mindset has far-reaching effects:

- **Personal Fulfillment:** There's an immense sense of fulfillment that comes from helping others. Witnessing the growth and success of those you've mentored brings a sense of pride and accomplishment.

- **Creating a Culture of Support:** By actively participating in mentorship, we foster a culture of learning and support. This culture, in turn, encourages others to engage in mentorship, creating a virtuous cycle of growth and giving.

- **Expanding Impact:** The impact of mentorship and support extends beyond the immediate relationship. Each individual you help is likely to pay it forward, amplifying the positive impact across the community.

Cultivating a network of support and engaging in mentorship are not just strategies for resilience; they are pillars of a thriving professional life. They bring depth and richness to our experiences, open doors to new possibilities, and allow us to contribute meaningfully to the lives of others. This interconnectedness of giving and receiving, learning and teaching, is what makes the journey of entrepreneurship not just successful but deeply rewarding.

Life Lesson 4: Taking Action

A defining trait of an unstoppable entrepreneur is the propensity to take decisive action. In both personal life and business, the difference between dreaming and achieving often boils down to one's willingness to act. I have learned that action is the bridge between ideas and realization, between potential and success. Taking action is fundamental, not just in overcoming hurdles but in seizing opportunities and realizing ambitions.

In my experience, the power of taking action manifests in various forms. It's about making those phone calls, setting up meetings, pitching ideas, and sometimes, it's about making tough decisions that could change the course of your business. Inaction, on the other hand, is a sure recipe for stagnation. It's easy to get caught in the loop of overthinking and planning, waiting for the 'perfect' moment. However, the truth is, that the perfect moment rarely arrives. Taking action, even in small steps, creates momentum and can lead to unexpected opportunities and growth.

In my personal life, taking action is equally crucial. Whether it's investing in self-care, pursuing a new hobby, or simply making time for family and friends, these actions contribute significantly to our overall well-being and satisfaction. For me, taking action meant investing in myself and joining that first multi-author collaboration book. That decision opened new doors in my career. It also involved me reaching out the the activity directors at local retirement homes and offering to teach acrylic paint classes. This activity brings immense joy not only to the residents but to me as well.

Taking action has a ripple effect. When we take action, we not only move closer to our goals but also inspire others around us to do the same. It sets a precedent, especially in a leadership role, demonstrating courage and determination. In business, this can translate to a motivated team, innovative solutions, and a dynamic work environment.

Integrating the principle of taking action into our resilience strategy adds a dynamic layer to our entrepreneurial journey. It's about not just bouncing back from setbacks but actively moving forward towards our goals. This proactive approach is what separates successful entrepreneurs from the rest. It's about understanding that resilience is not just about enduring but also about flourishing through decisive actions.

Taking action, therefore, is more than just a life lesson; it's a life strategy. It's the fuel that powers our journey, the force that turns dreams into reality. As we continue to navigate the complex waters of entrepreneurship, let us remember the power of action. Let's embrace it not just as a response to challenges but as a habitual practice in our daily lives, both personal and professional.

Embracing the Journey

These life lessons are not just abstract concepts but practical strategies that have shaped my entrepreneurial journey. They are the pillars that have supported me in my quest to be an unstoppable force in the face of adversity.

In addition to these lessons, it's essential to remember that resilience is a dynamic quality. It evolves as we face new challenges and grow. It requires constant nurturing through self-care, learning, and adaptability. As female entrepreneurs, we must remain vigilant in cultivating this quality, not just for our success but for the success of those we inspire and lead.

The journey of the female entrepreneur is emblematic of resilience. It's a testament to the strength, determination, and unyielding spirit that women bring to the table. As we navigate our paths, we become beacons of resilience, not just in our businesses but in our communities and families.

We stand as examples that despite the odds, with the right mindset, tools, and support, it is possible to overcome challenges and emerge stronger. Our stories become narratives of hope and inspiration for other women embarking on their entrepreneurial journeys.

Being an unstoppable female entrepreneur is about embracing the full spectrum of experiences - the successes, the failures, and everything in between. It's about building resilience, not just as a defense mechanism but as a proactive strategy for growth and success. It's about leading by example, showing the world the power and potential of the resilient female spirit.

As we forge ahead, let us carry these lessons close to our hearts, using them to fuel our journeys, inspire others, and create a legacy of strength, resilience, and unstoppable success.

Sally Larkin Green

Sally Larkin Green is the Vice President of Author Development at Action Takers Publishing. With a background in business and Christian mentorship, Sally's passion for storytelling and empowering others has transformed her into a bestselling author and inspirational speaker.

In March 2020, Sally realized that while she was good at caring for everyone else, she was really bad at caring for herself. This revelation sparked a journey of self-care, leading her to invest in herself and contribute to a multi-author book project. That experience ignited Sally's passion for writing and her desire to help others share their stories with the world.

As Vice President of Author Development, Sally guides aspiring writers through the process of transforming their ideas into bestselling books. She provides invaluable feedback, accountability, and encouragement.

Beyond her publishing role, Sally is a sought-after inspirational speaker, sharing her experiences and insights. She motivates individuals to embrace self-care, pursue their passions, and unleash their inner author.

Connect with Sally at

https://www.ActionTakersPublishing.com

CHAPTER 3
Life After Fear, My Unstoppable Journey

by Adele Rose

I wish to thank my husband and best friend Nick for our 50-year marriage together. Our bond never waned even when fear kept me hostage. His belief in my dreams inspired me to pursue my career without judgment but only in faith, love, and compassion. For that, I have been truly blessed.

In the captivating narrative of my life, I have embraced the role of an unstoppable and fearless female entrepreneur, charting a course through the intricate landscape of business and personal development. My journey is an embodiment of unwavering determination and an insatiable appetite for success, fueled by a relentless pursuit of self-discovery and professional achievement. In this captivating voyage, I have harnessed the power of personal development to unlock my fullest potential, dismantling the barriers that stood in my path. As I share my story, I invite you to join me in the exploration of a path defined by resilience, courage, and a relentless commitment to rewriting the rules. My narrative stands as a testament to the transformative might of self-belief, and I am thrilled to share this chapter of my journey with you.

As I sit here writing my book, I can't help but reflect on the winding path that led me here. Peeling back the layers of my past, I revisit the countless hurdles, deep-seated hurts, and persistent fears that have marked my journey through life. Now, as I stand as an entrepreneur, I recognize the significance of each trial and tribulation that has shaped my story. Since the 1990s, I have owned and operated a multitude of businesses, experiencing the highs of success and the lows of failures, but always persevering toward my goal of independence and authenticity. No longer tethered to the directives of corporate figures or the whims of a boss, I can proudly proclaim that I never gave up. Today, I find myself fulfilling my life's purpose as an intuitive spiritual reader and coach, extending a helping hand to those who find themselves paralyzed by fear or stuck in the mire of indecision. It is a realization that fills me with profound gratitude and a sense of being truly blessed.

In crafting my narrative, I have sought to reach out to those who, like me, have grappled with self-doubt and a lack of self-esteem. The individuals who question their purpose and worth, uncertain of their place in this vast universe. Some of us have convinced ourselves that we are too feeble, too inept to chase after our entrepreneurial dreams, and too timid to step into the shoes of a CEO. The mere thought of carving our own path in this intricate world seems beyond our reach, and for some, it remains a distant and unattainable fantasy. And yet, in each one of us, there lies a silent longing to succeed, an unspoken yearning to manifest the best version of ourselves, to turn our dreams into tangible realities. However, this yearning, this innate desire, often remains dormant until we summon the courage to ignite it. It is a manifestation of our unyielding will and determination, a testament to the depth of our desires and how fiercely we pursue them.

As I take a trip down memory lane, I find myself transported to my formative years in the 1960s, a time when I was an overweight, introverted teenager, devoid of any thoughts of business, just wanting to have fun in school and be a normal teenager. Unfortunately, I was robbed of that luxury by having to battle a debilitating and paralyzing disease, agoraphobia at the age of 14. This left me homebound, experiencing panic attacks and anxiety on a daily basis, but that, my friends is in another book. It was the crazy hippy era, marked by the absence of our modern conveniences of today like cell phones and the internet, an age where the intricacies of our day-to-day lives were orchestrated manually, through phone books, landlines, and payphones. Amidst the absence of technological luxuries, communication was characterized more by yelling than heartfelt conversations, and within the confines of my household, verbal outbursts often supplanted meaningful dialogue. In the midst of this loud environment, my mother's earnest desire for me to shed my excess weight became her obsession. It fueled a relentless pursuit of every diet, every weight loss pill, and every exercise regimen in a bid to attain the elusive ideal of thinness that society upheld. Mini skirts were the "in" thing, but sadly I never had the privilege of wearing them. My love for food, bordering with my mother's fixation on my weight, painted a vivid picture of the struggles I grappled with during those formative years.

At the tender age of seventeen, I made a conscious decision to embark on a transformative journey, birthing a meticulously designed diet plan that helped me shed an astonishing seventy-five pounds. The journey, while transformative, was not without its own set of challenges. The physical transformation that ensued was met with a startling realization, as I found myself face-to-face with a protruding bone on my leg, a sight that sent shivers down my spine. It was not until that moment that I realized the bone was my knee, a revelation that epitomized the extent of my disconnect with my own body.

The process of overcoming my battle with agoraphobia and ongoing fear, anxiety, and panic attacks proved to be a defining chapter in my personal narrative, a chapter that taught me to view fear through a different lens. It was a pivotal moment that underscored the profound impact of personal determination and resilience, igniting a flame within me that refused to be snuffed out. I faced it, found a way through it, and finally, I was free like a bird out of a cage! I socialized, had fun, and even was in a dance recital on stage, imagine that! I got married and had children but inside of me, something was missing. Although I was happy being a

Mom, I never felt whole. Staying home again felt like I was a prisoner again, so I made up my mind to get a job. I can do this, but what do I do? I planned for my children to go to daycare and the stage was set. My husband was not too thrilled, financially it would be a struggle, but I knew in my heart I would make it work! I was ready and determined! And so, when an opportunity to assume the role of manager at a health club presented itself through a newspaper advertisement, I found myself at a crossroads. I grappled with doubts and uncertainties, yet the possibility of success emboldened me. I seized the opportunity, venturing into uncharted territory, determined to carve a niche for myself in an unfamiliar landscape.

My job at the health club offered a panoramic view of the intricate dynamics that underpin successful business operations. I dived headfirst into the intricacies of management, dedicating myself wholeheartedly to steering the establishment toward greater heights. Long hours, relentless effort, and unwavering commitment characterized my tenure, as I assumed the role of a troubleshooter, navigating the challenges that threatened to derail the club's progress. However, as the club flourished under my guidance, I grappled with a gnawing dissatisfaction, a deep-seated unease that stemmed from my discontent with the hierarchical structure of corporate dynamics. The notion of contributing to the financial prosperity of an establishment while tethered to the directives of faceless executives and managerial directives left me yearning for more.

This yearning for more propelled me toward the realm of entrepreneurship, ultimately leading me to own and operate two health clubs for 14 years, each catering to a diverse clientele. The clubs were family-run with an additional staff of over 55 employees. The 11,000 square foot space was an all-women's and another 22,000 square foot was a muscle gym. We had personal training, classes, a boxing rink, tai chi, aerobics, diet counseling, etc. All very well-rounded to fit the needs of the time. The journey of entrepreneurship, while fraught with its own set of challenges, ushered in a newfound sense of fulfillment, a realization that I was destined for more than the confines of a standard corporate setup. The allure of entrepreneurship lies in its potential to merge my business keenness with a genuine desire to make a meaningful impact on the lives of my clients. It was a journey marked by the triumphs of human perseverance, as I bore witness to the transformative power of dedication and unwavering commitment.

In the pursuit of my passion for holistic wellness, I found myself drawn to the intimate intricacies of human struggles, whether it pertained to weight management, interpersonal relationships, or the nuances of overcoming deep-seated fears and anxieties. My experiences equipped me with a unique vantage point, one that stemmed from a place of deep empathy and an unwavering commitment to the well-being of those around me. I found myself assuming the role of a mentor, a guide, and an empathetic listener, drawing upon my personal struggles and triumphs to offer guidance and support to those in need. It was a role that resonated deeply with my sense of purpose, serving as a conduit for my desire to effect meaningful change in the lives of those who sought my guidance.

In the pre-pandemic era, the shifting landscape of technological advancements and the paradigm of online entrepreneurship posed a unique set of challenges. As someone with a limited understanding of the intricacies of modern technology, I grappled with the nuances of digital marketing and the complexities of establishing a robust online presence. My skepticism toward the disingenuous tactics employed by certain marketing entities underscored my commitment to authenticity and integrity, principles that I held in high regard. The challenges posed by my cognitive limitations, stemming from a prior encounter with carbon monoxide poisoning, served as a saddening reminder of the fragility of the human mind and the profound impact of external factors on our cognitive well-being.

Amidst the complications of uncertainties, a moment of introspection and prayer offered a glimmer of hope, ushering in a newfound sense of direction and purpose. It was during this period that I stumbled upon an opportunity that aligned perfectly with my innate gifts and passions. A door opened, leading me into the world of Tarot Arts, Intuitive Spiritual Guidance, Coaching, and Counseling. Drawn to the mystique of tarot from my early years, I found solace in the intricate symbolism and the depth of spiritual insight that the cards offered.

What struck me as particularly touching was the realization that my struggles and triumphs had equipped me with a unique perspective, one that allowed me to bridge the gap between spiritual guidance and personal transformation. Embracing my intuitive abilities and my unwavering commitment to authentic service, I found myself navigating the realms of spiritual intuition and empathic guidance, extending a helping hand to those grappling with the complexities of life and the entanglement of their emotions.

In each session, as I intertwined my energy with that of my clients, I discovered an unspoken language of the soul, a silent resonance that underscored the profundity of human experiences and the universal quest for clarity and understanding. It is a revelation that emphasizes the interconnectedness of our journeys, and the ways in which our paths intersect, creating a tapestry of shared experiences and collective growth.

Through the use of tarot as a tool, I channeled the energies of the universe, interpreting the messages that emerged with a deep sense of reverence and empathy. It is never about foreseeing the future or delving into the realm of the unknown; rather, it is about illuminating the path ahead, offering insights and guidance that facilitate a deeper understanding of the self and the world around us.

My work has its roots in love, light, and spiritual guidance, and I am Blessed in the foundation of the sacred realms of faith and belief. I recognized the transformative power of unconditional love and the profound impact of compassionate guidance. It was a philosophy that found its roots in the teachings of the Divine Intelligence, in the unwavering presence of Mother Mary, Jesus, and the Holy Spirit. I find solace in the timeless words of the "Our Father" prayer and the healing resonance of the HO'OPONOPONO prayer, each guiding me along the path of spiritual enlightenment and communal healing.

As I traverse the intricate pathways of spiritual guidance and empathic service, I remain steadfast in my commitment to authenticity and integrity. My work is a reflection of my unwavering belief in the innate goodness that resides within each of us, a testament to the transformative power of love and the profound impact of compassionate support. I stand as a beacon of hope and guidance, a humble conduit for the universal energies that bind us together and propel us toward greater heights of self-discovery and communal understanding.

If you find yourself at a crossroads, grappling with the complexities of life and the uncertainties that lie ahead, remember that you are not alone. Know that there is a guiding light, a source of unwavering support and empathic guidance that is only a phone call or an email away. My commitment to your well-being and personal growth remains unwavering, and it is my profound honor to accompany you on this sacred journey of self-discovery and spiritual transformation. You are not alone, and together, we can illuminate the path ahead, navigating the complexities of life with grace, compassion, and unwavering faith.

Believe in this below, because it speaks only truth:

"The feeling of success as an entrepreneur is an indescribable blend of exhilaration, fulfillment, and a profound sense of achievement. It's the culmination of relentless dedication, countless sleepless nights, and unwavering commitment to a vision. The moment when your efforts materialize into tangible results, when your business endeavors begin to flourish, is a testament to the power of perseverance and the unwavering belief in your own capabilities. It's a realization that transcends monetary gains, encompassing the profound satisfaction of creating something from nothing, of nurturing an idea into a thriving enterprise. The feeling of success as an entrepreneur is an affirmation of your resilience, creativity, and ability to navigate the complexities of the business landscape. It's a validation of your courage to defy conventional norms and carve your unique path in the world of commerce."

To all the kind souls who have taken the time to read this book, I extend my heartfelt gratitude and appreciation. Your willingness to delve into the pages of my story fills me with a profound sense of humility and joy. It is my sincerest hope that the words within these chapters resonate with you, touching your heart and inspiring you to move forward in your own unique journey. Life can be a labyrinth of challenges, but within each challenge lies the potential for growth and transformation. My wish is that this narrative serves as a beacon of hope, a reminder that, like me, you possess strength.

Love & Light,

Adele Rose

Adele Rose

Intuitive & Empathic Spiritual Creator, Entrepreneur and Coach, Adele Rose today lives a wonderful and spiritual life in Long Island, New York. Surrounded by her animals as an animal rescuer in Saving Homeless Pets for over 16 years, she lives a life free from fear, empowered by God and Blessed with a Divine gift to help others.

Adele has 3 children, 10 grandchildren, 2 great grandchildren and a husband of 50 years. She loves walking in nature, gardening, Tarot Arts, Mentoring, reading and her Spiritual Community of friends. Adele considers herself authentic in her business & personal life, living with Integrity & truth.

Although not currently active, Adele is a Licensed Practical Nurse for over 40 years. Her knowledge in the medical field continues to broaden the landscape in her business.

Connect with Adele at www.adelerosetarot.com.

CHAPTER 4
The Four Words That Changed My Life

by Alice Dartnell

Dedicated to my ex-husband!

"I want a divorce."

No sentence has more potential to kill a planned date night. Okay, so it was not the most exciting of date nights—a night in, with fajitas and a movie—but I didn't think my fajitas were that bad. To be fair, it was September 2020, and we were still in and out of lockdown in the UK, so our options were limited.

No one goes into a marriage expecting to hear those words. In a split second, my entire world as I knew it, and had worked so hard to create, suddenly came crashing down.

My mind instantly went through a million questions and thoughts, from fear (My life is screwed!) to social embarrassment (What will I tell people?) to the absolutely, insignificantly, ridiculous (Are we still making fajitas for dinner because I got all the ingredients out?)

Despite the world-shattering announcement, this wasn't actually the beginning of the end. The next day, he said that maybe his decision "was too hasty," seeing as we had been together ten years. He asked for a 'trial separation.' You'll do anything to save your marriage so, of course, I agreed. Six months, no contact or communication. He needed to, "Go find himself," he said. In hindsight, this turned out to be BS, but I am not here to badmouth him.

In comparison to going through the actual divorce, this was the hardest part of the experience. I think being in limbo is worse than going through it. Was I married? Was he coming back? Should I take the photos of us down from the walls? Should I keep the wedding ring on? Should I take his stuff out of the wardrobe? I had to take the car for a service a few days after his leaving and burst into uncontrollable tears when the guy at the garage innocently said, "So your husband has booked the car in …" Was he … my husband?

Shortly after the trial separation began, the UK went into another lockdown. In retrospect, this did me a favour, because I just wanted to focus on myself and my business and hole myself away from the busyness of real life whilst going through all of this.

The truth is, I had already hit a couple of bumps in the road starting my business. Despite the emotional devastation, I was also weirdly determined to make sure this was not going to bulldoze me and my business dreams.

The business false start and burnout

I started the business just before the UK went into the first lockdown. I had been in Mexico with my dad for a couple of weeks at the end of February 2020, fleshing out my business plans and ideas—what did I want my business to look like? What was my mission? How was I going to bring in clients?

My business would be in-person and face-to-face. That was the primary way I would market and work with my clients. As I lived in London, this seemed perfect! I remember landing on Friday 13th March 2020. By Monday, the country was in lockdown.

Within a matter of days of starting my business, I was already back to the drawing board thinking about how to 'pivot' the business (needing to pivot—a popular pandemic phrase!)

And now this bombshell—"I want a divorce."

Starting a business is hard enough, let alone when you suddenly find that the very person you thought was your teammate and rock abandons you six months after the start. I had no idea how I was going to do it.

It was no longer a case of 'I want to make it work,' but I HAD to make it work.

After I gave up corporate, he was the breadwinner, and we had agreed that he would financially support me for a few years whilst I got the business up and running. I had to be realistic that no matter how much I wanted to save my marriage, there was a huge possibility that he might not come back. This business had to work! People were being furloughed in the UK in every industry (did anyone know what the word furloughed even meant before the pandemic?) I could not go back to corporate, even if I wanted to (and I definitely didn't want to, by the way).

I had officially registered the business on 1st February 2019. A couple of months later, my excitement and big vision were quickly squashed when I had a crashing burnout. So, within months of pursuing the dream I had had since I was a teenager, I had to make the tough decision … do I press pause before I've even truly begun?

It was a Tuesday morning in June, about six a.m., I don't know what the driver was, but I went downstairs whilst my husband was getting ready for work, and suddenly blurted out the words, "Something bad is going to happen." I told him that I had this awful feeling that disaster was looming—either I was going to be in a terrible accident, or I was going to stab him! Don't ask me where that came from, but the fact I blurted it out is clearly an indicator that I wasn't in a good place. Just for the record though, I do not think he left me because he was fearful that I was actually going to stab him! He's an ex-marine. He could have well handled himself had I wielded a kitchen knife at him!

A couple of days later, it hit me what was wrong.

Burnout. In an ideal world, I would have stepped back, and taken some time out to go within and stay quiet to allow myself to recover. However, 2019 was the year all my girlfriends decided to get married. I had six weddings in less than 12 months, three in which I had a crucial role to play and a big involvement, as I was a bridesmaid!

So, at a time when my body was desperately crying out for rest and recovery, I had the most hectic social calendar ever! I remember landing from one bachelorette party abroad on Tuesday morning, and then taking off for another on Friday!

I made the conscious decision that I would be willing to delay my recovery by pushing on with the social plans, press pause on the business and attempt it again in 2020.

Whilst I am happy with that decision, 2019 was also one of my hardest years. I genuinely felt like a shell. I was trying to put on this happy face for everyone, but deep down inside, I felt like I was never going to get Alice back. I thought she had gone forever. And do you know what? She was.

The time management obsession

One of the big contributors to my burnout was my obsession with time management—to be specific, it was my obsession with maximising my time.

I suffered from severe depression, an eating disorder and low self-worth when I was in my teens which, unfortunately, crippled me for a decade. When I started to recover from this, I realised how much time I had wasted. I dread to calculate the number of precious hours I wasted crying and criticising myself. I hated everything about myself. I would spend hours sitting in front of the mirror, scrutinizing my body and my looks.

Also, growing up, I had a difficult relationship with my mum. She is from the tiny island of Okinawa, Japan, and the difference in our backgrounds, cultures and how people express their love is vastly different. The fact that we can't speak each other's language is something I am reminded of when we have daily miscommunications even now. I found all of this very overwhelming and challenging in my teens, which contributed to my depression.

When I started to recover in 2010, I realised I was more in control of my life than just my circumstances. I started to get out of my 'victim mindset' mentality, became obsessed with personal development and vowed to never waste another minute of my time ever again!

Like all good obsessions, I took this to the extreme! In my bid to not waste time, I became fixated on productivity. I was always rushing. I wanted to maximise every waking minute, so I was often multi-tasking and I struggled to switch off, relax or always be present. I started getting up earlier and going to bed later to try and cram more into my day. I thought I was doing the right thing maximizing my time but all I was doing was leading myself to a burnout.

I mentioned that going through burnout was one of the worst experiences I've had because I genuinely thought I would never get Alice back. I was right. I didn't.

The burnout broke me, but a better Alice emerged out of it. It was going through the burnout that made me realise that the way I had been previously living was not sustainable or healthy. And this is what led me to create my own time management systems around "Energy Management."

I'm grateful for going through that horrendous experience because it has led me to create a business that I am so passionate about today. My passion is helping others create their own, "Life by Design" and teaching time management through energy management and mindset. Had I not gone through the burnout, I would be teaching time management all wrong. For me, the 'traditional' methods I had grown up with, along with the 'hustle culture' and the motivational videos shouting at you to 'sleep when you're dead,' did not work.

I thought I was great at time management—I was organised, planned, punctual, and could juggle multiple projects. I even finished work at five p.m. every day and made time for things like kickboxing training and charity work.

I learnt the hard way that time management isn't only about managing your time, but also about managing your energy. A tough experience but that is now fuel, passion, and inspiration to help others. In the last couple of years, I have grown a business internationally teaching and coaching hundreds of people these principles I now live by. Through coaching and consultancy, with my own courses and programmes, as a guest speaker and writer … I can just sit back and think, had I not gone through the burnout in 2019, I wouldn't be doing this.

Getting through the divorce

My principles in "energy management" are some of the things that got me through the dark times of the divorce.

I decided that I couldn't control what happened to me, but I could control what I did next. I wanted to cultivate my positive energy, so whenever I felt the rage rise, I would close my eyes and "send him love" (a technique I learnt from Gabby Bernstein) and remind myself that I wanted to, "act with grace" throughout all of this. Do not get me wrong I'm no saint and the various holes that I punched in the kitchen wall show that!

There would be days (probably every day) that I would cry on the sofa for hours and hours. I felt so lost, confused, scared and angry. The "time management freak," as I like to call her, still lurks within me. She was raging inside, angry at the fact that not only had he walked out, but he had stolen that time from me.

I didn't want to be wasting time—crying on the sofa, feeling exhausted and lying awake with sleepless nights. I wanted to get my business up and running, but I couldn't work to my full capacity, so I felt more time was being robbed from me. This taught me a valuable lesson that I brought into my business, and I teach as well. Being productive and progressing in your goals doesn't just come down to time and how many hours you work each day.

I realised even more so, that it wasn't just about time but also energy—physical, mental, spiritual, and emotional. I worked on my energy on all fronts, from hiring a Personal Trainer to working with a therapist, learning more about quantum physics and understanding how our bodies work, making time for meditation, journaling, breathwork and anything else that would help me holistically. This taught me a valuable lesson that I brought into my business, and I teach as well. Being productive and progressing in your goals doesn't just come down to time and how many hours you work each day.

Now, I teach others what I know about 'Energy Management,' and it goes beyond just the time management practices. I teach things like planning, being organized, having systems, etc., but I also support clients with their energy management on everything from gut health, moon cycles, how the body functions, cognitive function, and focus, as well as traditional time management principles. Over the years, my expertise has continued to grow as I devour more information about what contributes to our energy (I have a healthier obsession now!)

Trust, self-belief, and self-worth played a huge part in getting through all of this. Every day, I worked hard at developing this and creating a strong mindset, trying to see little snips of evidence saying that I was worthy. From keeping screenshots of all the lovely messages clients sent me about how much I was helping them, to the positive feedback I would receive from people in workshops I didn't know, or plastering the house with positive affirmations (seriously, the bathroom mirror was covered with post-it notes).

Knowing my values helped me through the separation and the divorce—I aligned myself with the things that matter to me, like health, learning, adding value to others' lives, having fun, creating memories, etc. Every morning, I would meditate and journal, and ask myself, "What am I doing today to work on my own goals, values, and life by design? What do I need to do to develop my business and how can I provide value for my clients?"

Was any of this easy? Of course not. Every day was a conscious effort. But the hard work paid off. I didn't just survive—I grew through all of this, and I also doubled the size of my business in the second year despite everything that was going on in my personal life.

A new chapter

I feel like this is just the beginning. The divorce wrapped up in February 2022, and within three weeks of that, I was on a flight to Valencia, Spain. It wasn't in the life plans, but I found myself single and no longer a homeowner, so I wanted to make the most of this and see it as an opportunity. Whilst I adore London, I wanted a change of scenery, to tick off some major bucket list items and in addition, to push my comfort zone and challenge myself. This is why I enrolled in a language school in Spain to learn Spanish—a lifelong dream. Also, I pushed myself by going to a country where I didn't speak the language (except for a few things like "un vino blanco") and didn't have any connections. Friends asked that considering I had just gone through the hardest of things, why was I deliberately doing something so challenging? But the divorce hadn't been my choice. I needed to show myself I could push my comfort zone on my own terms too!

This amazing experience in 2022 was followed by the most incredible 10-week travel adventure in South America with one of my oldest friends at the start of 2023. I am so grateful to her, as I just tagged along on the trip she had already booked. Her words hit me, "If you don't come now, when will you go?" This had been an item on my bucket list for 20 years!

I am a big believer in turning "pain into power" and making the most of the situation you are in. Now, I would have never been the one to call for a divorce, but seeing where I have found myself, I'm determined to make it work for me.

The doors are now closed on the "Post-Divorce Sabbatical" chapter (the 15 months I took out for Valencia and South America), and I am ready for the next instalment. This one is about healing, growth, travel and building my business empire—my "Life by Design." This is so much more than a snazzy tagline I use in my business. It is something I want to embody every single day and empower others to do so, too. I want to live my life on my terms, making choices every day that are right for me, and using my time as I want. I want to get moving on those bucket list dreams that have been sitting there idle for way too long.

I will level with you; I am not where I thought I would be at 37. Had you told me five years ago that

I would be single, a digital nomad without my own home, and running an international business, I would have thought you were crazy. It's vastly different from the identity and life I had as a wife, homeowner and working in a corporate office in London!

At the time of this writing, I am currently living in Cambodia. I have always wanted to live abroad, but this wasn't ever on the list! In fact, I always said I would hate to live here and didn't understand why my parents have lived between here and the UK for so long! But one of the things I have learnt over the last few years is to stay open and flexible, as you don't know what is around the corner and what opportunities are there.

I decided to move here temporarily after Spain and the South American sabbatical to be closer to my mum. We're working hard on our relationship and for the first time ever we're starting to really understand and get to know one another. I'm learning Japanese and healing the deep wounds.

Is life perfect? Of course not. But I am excited for the future and have huge dreams and ambitions for myself and my business.

Almost daily, I think about all that happened, and my heart breaks for past Alice. I wish I could go back to her, though, and tell her, "It is going to be ok. You've got this."

During the divorce, when Cambodia finally lifted its travel restrictions, my dad flew back to the UK to help me out. I was so excited the day he was due to arrive, that someone was coming to rescue me. But then I had the realisation—there was no knight in shining armour coming to rescue me. I was my own knight in shining armour! I had to rescue myself.

"I want a divorce." Those four words that changed my life forever. I now feel more settled mentally, emotionally, and spiritually than I have in the last five years. I am not deluded in thinking that life isn't going to throw me a curve ball at any moment, but when it does, I will be okay. As my motto goes, "When life throws you a lemon, make the best damn lemonade you can." Whatever happens, I am ready. I am unstoppable.

Alice Dartnell

Alice is a life and success coach on a mission to empower you to create a "Life by Design" (not by default!)

She is an expert in time management and productivity but teaches it through "Energy Management" and mindset. She takes a holistic approach to time management, teaching that time management is not just about managing your time, but also your energy!

She discovered this through her own personal journey following a burnout in 2019, despite being 'great at time management', realising that your energy—physical, mental, emotional, and spiritual—plays a huge part in how you use and maximise your time!

Alice's heritage is part-English and part-Japanese. She is originally from London but has been travelling the world working on her online business since 2022.

She offers 1-2-1 coaching privately and within organizations, as well as consultancy for companies looking to be more productive whilst supporting the well-being and development of their staff. She runs her own live group coaching programmes and created "Transform your Time," a unique online time management course combining online course content with live support and coaching.

She is also a speaker, appearing as a guest in various summits and podcasts, as well as an executive contributor for Brainz Magazine and other publications.

Connect with Alice at www.alicedartnell.com.

CHAPTER 5

Seasoned Strategies for Entrepreneurial Success

by Diana L. Howles

This chapter is dedicated to Thomas A. and Joan J.

Unstoppable. Fearless. When you first hear these words, they may sound beyond reach or even impossible. But to be fearless doesn't mean the absence of fear. To me, it means that even if you feel trepidation about taking an action—like starting your own business—you do it anyway. You research the market, take calculated risks, and see where it leads. I also believe you don't need to be a superhero to be unstoppable. You just need to find a way to keep moving forward.

I liken the journey of a solopreneur or entrepreneur to competitive hurdles in track and field events. One after another, athletes attempt to clear each hurdle while racing to the finish line. The same can be said for an entrepreneur's journey. Inevitably, business owners will encounter barriers along the way. Sure, there are achievements as well, but encountering obstacles is also part of the package. The key is not only how we work to resolve each of those challenges, but also, how we react to them. That's what makes us unstoppable.

In my own business at Howles Associates, we certainly have encountered our share of challenges over the years. Yet through the highs and lows, we learned to adapt, be agile, and keep moving forward. We tried to learn from our mistakes and apply the lessons learned for next time. Through it all, I learned several key strategies. It is my hope that sharing five of these strategies will help you act fearlessly as well.

1. Look for Opportunity in Adversity
2. Narrow Your Niche
3. Leverage Global Resources

4. Surround Yourself with Personal Advisors
5. Trust Your Gut

Strategy #1: Look for Opportunity in Adversity

The idea for launching a business first surfaced when I faced a major barrier in my professional career. At the time, I worked for a financial services company as a learning designer, trainer, and consultant. As part of a major corporate restructuring, our entire Learning & Development Department, which consisted of 50 plus employees, was laid off. The timing of the layoff was a bit surreal for me, because at that point I had worked there a total of seven years, seven months, and seven days! In some cultures, the number seven means complete. So, I took it as a sign that my employment there was now complete.

What's interesting about endings is they can also birth beginnings. Not knowing what my next steps would be, my husband was the first to suggest we consider starting a business from scratch. I remember being excited about the prospect, but worried about whether it would pay the bills. I did like the flexibility that owning a business would afford me as a mom, especially since I had a toddler at home at the time.

And so, we used that layoff to catapult our own LLC a few months later. We made the leap even though I had fears about how to create a website, market to new clients, and secure enough work. But we launched anyway, and 17 years later, we're still going strong.

Another example of looking for opportunity in adversity came with the devastating and tragic COVID-19 pandemic. In my line of work, conference presentations and speaking bookings were appropriately cancelled to prevent the spread of infection and save lives. As everything rapidly moved online, I suddenly realized a new opportunity to help people.

As a pioneer of live online training, I had two decades of experience with online facilitation and had trained virtual employees all over the world using virtual training platforms. I realized, now more than ever, global professionals needed guidance on how to effectively facilitate live online training, develop on-camera presence, and engage virtual participants. Previously, I had submitted a few book proposals but was told no from various publishers. So, I tried once more a few months after the pandemic first began, and this time, it was accepted. That book, *Next Level Virtual Training: Advance Your Facilitation* (ATD Press, 2022) went on to win multiple awards and become an Amazon best seller. Many practitioners across the globe have let me know how much it's helped them, and the entire journey has been incredibly rewarding.

So, when plans dissolve, we have a choice. The sooner we can look for "what can I do?" instead of "what can't I do?" the more resilient we'll be, and the more likely it will be that opportunities will present themselves. We just need to be open to new possibilities to see them.

Strategy #2: Narrow Your Niche

One common mistake I often see new entrepreneurs and solopreneurs making is one that I've also made myself. It can be very tempting for new business owners to try to offer too many services. For example, instead of finding a niche and marketing your business as the "evaluation experts," for example, you decide to also provide leadership development courses, data management training, consulting on learning management systems, design eLearning tutorials, and develop performance support tools. Do you see the dilemma?

Some clients may think you don't have a specialty because of the wide spectrum of services. Clients are left to wonder where your real expertise lies. For example, do you specialize in leadership development, or data management, or evaluation? How could you possibly be skilled at them all? It can be confusing to understand what you do well. So, when you try to be everything to everybody, the perception is you become a master of none.

Over the last several years as our business has evolved, we've learned to narrow our niche as well. As proof of this evolution, our business website has been revamped many times. In the beginning, our services focused on instructional technology and multimedia for eLearning design and development. Now, we are live online training specialists who help professionals facilitate effective virtual training programs.

Do your best to focus your business on one or a few core specialties instead. Imagine for a moment that your home furnace stopped working. You'd likely hire a furnace repair company that specializes in fixing furnaces, right? You wouldn't just trust the repair to a general contractor. So, narrow your niche out of the gate and allow your declared expertise to be your brand and boost your business.

Strategy #3: Leverage Global Resources

When you're first launching your business, it makes sense to do most of the work yourself, especially if you're a solopreneur. As you begin to grow, it can be tempting to continue to do all the work yourself, as you may think this saves you money. As women, we may have the tendency to take on more than what we should at home and at work as we try to "have it all." But once your business expands, it's time to leverage other resources to assist you. This is an essential principle that will help your business grow.

This is one mistake we made when we initially tried to do too much ourselves. Although there were lean times too, there were also times when we were overwhelmed with work. I remember feeling completely exhausted while working on projects late into the nights and on most weekends during that time. From a financial perspective, you might reflect on those years and say we were successful. But because I was so burned out, I don't view that period as a success. It placed stress on my relationships, and I was depleted. You must decide what success looks like for you. The older version of me views success differently now. We try to outsource more so we can manage a workload that prioritizes family time, down time, well-being, getting enough sleep, and physical fitness. These are my new non-negotiables.

Fortunately, with the affordances of today's technology, global resources are accessible with the click of a button. Many of my friends who are business owners in Australia and other countries employ Virtual

Assistants (VAs) to assist them. In our business, we've sub-contracted with associates in Eastern Europe, a graphic artist in Idaho, learning designers in California and on the East Coast of the US, and more. In the past, we've worked with professionals in the Philippines to improve the search engine optimization (SEO) of our website. More recently, we've leveraged services like Fiverr International Ltd. to hire global freelancers. For example, we contracted a Social Media Marketing Manager in Albania to help us create content with messaging for social media posts. And we have partners in other support service areas such as website maintenance, lawyers, and accountants.

Leveraging artificial intelligence tools (AI) is another way to save you time and accelerate productivity. Look for ways to use ChatGPT, for example, and other large language models (LLM) like Google's Bard to generate text for you. With skilled prompt engineering, a specific, clear, detailed prompt equips AI to brainstorm ideas for your business, draft marketing pieces, write email replies, research books, or write article drafts. In our business, we use AI to write the rough draft for some of our pieces, and from there, correct errors and edit it ourselves to make it our own (NOTE: AI was not used to write this chapter).

The point is that to help your business grow, employ others to help with responsibilities that may not be your area of expertise, so you can focus on the things that are. Your productivity is limited to a certain number of hours every day, so be sure to look for creative ways to outsource, sub-contract, or hire to help you focus your time on what you do best.

Strategy #4: Surround Yourself with Personal Advisors

We've all benefitted from bouncing ideas off colleagues we respect or inviting people we admire to share their advice. Surrounding yourself with other female leaders, advisors, mentors, or accountability partners you meet with regularly can be very helpful.

I meet monthly via Zoom with a fellow female author who lives in another state in the US. We keep each other accountable by sharing our goals for book marketing and our businesses. It's been great to celebrate each other's successes and encourage each other when we fall short. The beauty of having an accountability partner is that regardless of what comes your way, you both keep each other moving forward.

Another reason it's so important to surround yourself with other leaders—and other women leaders—is because in today's business world, gender differences in the workplace aren't always discussed in a forthright way. Connecting with other female business owners or professional women groups creates a space for women to discuss those gender differences and talk honestly with other women about their experiences as leaders in today's business world.

I was fortunate to keynote virtually for a UK conference where I was the final speaker. All the speakers before me were from the UK and male. I realized I stuck out because of my American accent, but also because I was the only female speaker. At my high school graduation, I too was the only female speaker and spoke last after two of my male peers. It's fortunate to be placed in the position as last speaker, but in both of those instances, I was also aware that it was advantageous to be the only woman speaker as it made me and my message more memorable.

In her book, *It's Not a Glass Ceiling, it's a Sticky Floor: Free Yourself from the Hidden Behaviors Sabotaging Your Career Success* (McGraw Hill, 2007), author Rebecca Shambaugh suggests female leaders form their own personal Board of Directors. This individual advisory group is there to serve you in a supportive role. You can adapt this concept as you best see fit. You can even meet with each of your hand selected advisors one-on-one to consult with them on various issues. Your personal board may include former colleagues, trusted friends, a parent, or other women leaders you admire.

When I was considering an idea for a new product launch, I asked three separate professional women out for coffee and let them know I wanted to seek their counsel. I have the deepest, professional respect for all of them. I presented my new business idea to each of them individually and asked for their feedback. To my surprise, the idea resonated with all of them, and they even expounded on my initial idea even more. So, consider surrounding yourself with advisors, mentors, or trusted female colleagues who can support where you want to go professionally by serving on your personal advisory panel.

Strategy #5: Trust Your Gut

Finally, then, my number one tip for becoming a fearless female entrepreneur is to trust your gut. A woman's intuition is golden. Although my fourth strategy highlights the importance of surrounding yourself with advisors to weigh multiple perspectives, it's *how* you proceed that is ultimately your decision.

Others may tell you your dream is far-fetched. People close to you may say launching a business will never happen, or family members may explain that the odds of achieving what you want are slim. But you and you alone know deep down that this is your dream and it's burning inside you. It's not the fault of others that they may not be on board. They don't have access to your intuition. They can't feel the craving or hear the calling. Only you can. Ultimately, you must follow what you know to be true for you.

Listening to my intuition has helped me in many business situations. In one instance, I was asked to deliver an in-person workshop to an organization's Talent Development Department at their client site. Our normal business protocol is to request the client meet us at least 30 minutes beforehand to move through any security reception and allow us to set up our technology and troubleshoot in the room. In this instance, however, the client said they were simply unable to allow early access and could only escort me 15 minutes before the workshop was to begin.

Now, if you've traveled across the country presenting workshops at client sites and conferences, you know that surprises often happen with your devices and the in-room equipment. Listening to my intuition, I knew that this wasn't a match made in heaven. Given that I wouldn't have a lot of time to troubleshoot, I opted to bring two laptops with me that day just in case. Sure enough, my modern laptop did not sync with the data projector in the room—even though I had brought adapters. As the start time for the workshop inched closer and attendees began to fill the room, I realized I needed to pivot and boot up my older laptop instead. Sure enough, my second laptop worked. It would have been easy to brush off my intuition with a thought like, "It'll be OK. You're just overthinking this," but I'm so thankful I listened to my instincts and brought two laptops that day. Your intuition is there for a reason. Listen to it.

Summary

In his book, *The Road Less Traveled* (Simon and Schuster, 2003) author M. Scott Peck writes, "Once we truly know that life is difficult—once we truly understand and accept it—then life is no longer difficult." This simple yet profound truth slices to the core. Once we adjust our expectations to be more aligned with reality, there is a mental shift that can free us. Our expectations become more realistic. The key is to bring eventual acceptance to new situations we find ourselves in, instead of getting stuck and resisting anything that doesn't fit with how we think things should be. But once we accept "what is," a path of greater ease often unfolds and ideas for solutions can begin to emerge.

This lesson is so applicable to my journey as an entrepreneur. Looking back over the years as the current

CEO, there were certainly times that were trying and joyful, lean and abundant, rocky and smooth. As the popular adage suggests, skilled sailors don't develop their skill sets with calm seas, but rocky seas. So, my recommendation to solopreneurs and entrepreneurs is to expect your journey to include both polarities (success and challenge), and to be ready.

I asked the legendary self-esteem expert and New York Times bestselling author, Jack Canfield, how he approaches situations which don't unfold the way you envision. Decades earlier, I had watched him masterfully continue speaking even when his slides stopped projecting in the middle of a keynote in front of 10,000 people. This took place at an international conference, and the data projector suddenly stopped working. Reflecting on those moments, he shared how he believes everything happens for a purpose and there's no point in freaking out. All you can do is your best, and he emphasizes that how we react during those times also significantly influences the outcome as well.

The key, of course, is to persevere through challenges, especially when you intuitively know you're on the right path. When hurdles appear in your racing lane—and they will—you find a way to go around them, over them, under them, move them to the side, break them down, or forge a new trail altogether. Overcoming barriers certainly can be challenging. But it's also where we grow the most. So, don't let a hurdle stop you in your tracks. The word unstoppable may sound "Impossible," but when you re-frame the word Impossible and add an apostrophe, it can also become "I'm possible."

To be the stunning, female entrepreneur that you were meant to be, remember to look for opportunity in adversity, narrow your niche, leverage global resources, surround yourself with personal advisors, and trust your gut.

And if you follow these five strategies, you'll quite simply be . . . unstoppable.

Diana L. Howles

Diana L. Howles is an award-winning speaker, Amazon best-selling author, and global virtual and hybrid training expert who brings over 20 years of experience in the learning industry.

As a world-class facilitator, she has led virtual programs in more than a dozen countries. She is author of the book, *Next Level Virtual Training: Advance Your Facilitation* (2022) which has won multiple awards, and is a contributing author to the #1 international bestseller, *Resilient Women in Life & Business* (2023).

As CEO of Howles Associates, LLC, Diana is a sought-after and popular speaker at international conferences and events.

Connect with Diana at
https://www.howlesassociates.com.

CHAPTER 6
Replace the Old Burden With the New Version of You

by Fari Eskandari Gonzaque

Dedicated to my mother and father ... If it wasn't for them, their strength, resilience, and love of serving, I would not have become the woman I am today. My mother always loved me unconditionally. My father's athleticism and power live on in me.

August 22, 1978

I was 21 years old, and I remember the plane taking off and thinking ... Oh, thank you, God! Yes, I was finally leaving Iran. I was running away from my dictator, father, and one of my brothers.

I had planned this ever since I was 17 years old. That very afternoon, my father slapped my face many, many times. He was very loving to the whole world, except not so with his own family. This was by no means an isolated incident. It happened many times. and that's when I decided to leave my family. I had to plan it cleverly and wait until I turned 21 because by then I didn't need to have my parents' consent for my passport to be issued.

After leaving Iran, I really thought I was going to be so free and so happy and everything was going to be so amazing, just as I wanted my life to be. Little did I know, that was the onset of all the difficulties and the problems because I wanted to start my life all by myself, on my own without anyone's help.

When we are young, we think we can do all things by ourselves, regardless of all the difficulties we have to go through. Isn't it amazing, I was not even 20 years old yet when I started my plan.

I was so sure when I got to the other side of the world that life was going to be fantastic and smiling at me day in and day out, but it was quite the contrary. I made up my mind that I needed to create the life that I wanted and not what my parents wanted for me. So, I put my armor on and thought I could fight anything in this world, only to prove to the world that I mattered, and I really did fight.

I remember the first week in London, my cousin and I were walking around, looking at the whole city, and looking at all the different people. I realized, "Wow, everybody is so slender and I was so fat … and huge. I was barely 5'5 and weighed 205 pounds.

I got my first job as an Au Pair just outside of London and it lasted for one year. At the time, I knew less than 10 words of English. Consequently, it was challenging to communicate with the family. I was only allowed to go to English classes for four hours a week. I had to find other, faster ways to learn English. My dictionary became my best friend. It was with me everywhere.

I was severely homesick, and it was getting worse. The feeling of loneliness was getting intense so I ate more and gained even more weight. My Scottish landlady, Sandra, was seven months pregnant with her second child and I weighed a lot more than her! One day I decided to lose weight, and Sandra offered to help and encourage me with my weight loss.

Nine months later, I lost 50 pounds. I went for long walks, ran, and swam every day before and after my shift as an au pair, practiced and pronounced out loud the new words I learned in English whilst exercising. I noticed very soon that my depression was subsiding. Oh wow, what could it be? Oh yes, working out and cutting out sugar, were the answers. Working out in any available format became my new medication to get rid of my depression. My friends didn't recognize me at first since I hadn't seen them for 11 months.

Soon after I left Iran, the revolution started in September 1978. I planned to get a Visa and move to the U.S., but with the chaos in Iran, every embassy closed its doors to the Iranians. Life became difficult, we couldn't find jobs anywhere. That was the onset of the turmoil in my life, as an Iranian girl, but I never stopped.

Due to all the hatred and animosity towards us, "No" was the answer when I applied for jobs. The more I pushed, the more I applied myself. I walked from one shop to another, asking for a job, any job, as long as I could earn money and find work to support myself.

By the time I was 27 years of age, I was diagnosed with a debilitating disease called Fibromyalgia. Every inch of me hurt. Even the roots of my hair were in so much pain. I remember combing my hair (which was very full and very long) to be very painful. But I kept on pushing through, working out, running, walking, and playing tennis. I wasn't going to let pain bring me down. I thought to myself, "I didn't leave Iran to come here to give up or fail because of my body aches," so I pushed through day in and day out.

Getting a Visa to stay in England was almost impossible. So, a few years later, I ended up getting married to my coworker just to obtain a Visa. It was a marriage of convenience. Despite being checked by immigration in the middle of the night and early in the morning, I finally got my permanent residency in England.

Needless to say, we divorced after I obtained my residency in England, and I married my boyfriend at the time, with whom I had lived for five years prior.

Our marriage lasted 20 months.

As a benefit of my citizenship, I managed to find great jobs as a fashion consultant in the best boutiques in London.

After many years of working for others, the idea occurred to me to open a boutique in London. I wondered what it would take to one day own my own boutique. It became an impossible dream for sure, but I didn't stop thinking and talking about it. I didn't have the means for it to come to fruition.

Despite everyone's discouragement of my dream, I decided to approach my bank manager, plead with him, and ask for his help. He had known me for quite a few years.

Yes! He approved his support for me to open my own shop, and everyone was surprised. How did I do it? And my answer was, "If you want something, keep working on it, and don't give up." In my speech, on the day of the grand opening, I said, "Take every 'No' as a gift, become stronger, and fight for whatever you want to achieve."

My business was successful for seven years, but even then I hadn't stopped dreaming about emigrating to America.

My success in England was short-lived. In 1990, the recession hit the world. It affected my business and I went bankrupt overnight. I believed the bankruptcy was a gift, so I could move to America free of any guilt. Since I was 15 years old, this has been my biggest dream.

Dec 8th, 1991

Despite everyone's discouraging advice, I finally gave my shop to a couple of my male friends, and in pursuit of my dream, I moved to the U.S. and started all over again. I was 34 years old.

At the time, I had two brothers living in Los Angeles. I flew there and lived between the two of them for close to four months.

My elder brother and my father were the main reasons I left Iran. Now, not having my own place, I had to stay with my elder brother in America. It was excruciating to be with him for those few months. I was desperate to move out of his home. I had no idea what I wanted to do with my career.

I knew I loved working out, exercising, playing tennis, and swimming, and they gave me the power to help deal with stress and depression.

I was worried and confused about choosing my career. I knew I didn't want to go back to fashion anymore so I kept praying, and asking for guidance. Finally, I received a message from a higher power.

The message was, "Fitness is my passion, and should be my career."

Shortly after I arrived in the U.S., I met my new friend, Chloe Davis who coincidentally, was British. I shared this divine message with my new friend. She was an aerobics instructor.

Chloe was a gift from heaven. She helped me get hired as a front desk receptionist in a very small Health Club in Brentwood, California. Working at the front desk was not satisfying but good enough to help me pay rent for a little studio apartment and move out of my brother's home. Once again, I felt the liberation I was dreaming about.

The next step was that I wanted to become a fitness trainer, but I didn't have a work permit. What do I do now? No Health Club would hire me as a fitness trainer. So, without my work permit, I ended up training people in their homes.

After a few months of searching, I met a lawyer who charged me $10,000 to get my permit. He said there would be no promises. There was so much paperwork involved for the documents I needed, but I was determined to get my green card. I was fortunate to get it with my British passport.

Despite all the discouraging remarks about my being Iranian during the conflict between America and Iran, it took two years, but I finally got my Green Card.

Whilst I was waiting for my Green Card status, a tragedy occurred. While driving myself and three friends from San Francisco to Los Angeles, I lost control of the car.

The accident resulted in my best friend Nikoo, becoming brain-dead. I was severely injured and thankfully the two other passengers were perfectly okay.

Needless to say, my depression hit the roof and the fibromyalgia in me got to its worst and I became suicidal.

To top it all off, I was sued by the family of my friend Nikoo. After a long conversation with their attorney, he decided to send me for medical tests at a UCLA medical facility in L.A. The tests lasted one week. It was determined that I had ADHD and dyslexia, which I had not been aware of. I didn't even know what those terms meant.

I was found not liable and it was decided that the incident was 100% accidental.

It took a massive toll on me emotionally, physically, and mentally, but I knew I couldn't stop looking for the lesson in all of this. Years later, I found my gift in this tragedy by choosing to be a fitness trainer/ life coach.

A few years after that tragedy, I earned my American citizenship. The sorrow and the sadness of the accident brought a huge question to mind. What was the lesson? The more I searched for an answer, the more I found out how many people suffer from ADHD, dyslexia, and fibromyalgia, and they go unnoticed, not loved, and not cared for.

Subsequently, I became very compassionate in my field, believing all the trauma I went through was to learn from and become a service to anyone else out there who was going through the same challenges I had. Ironically, no one would hire me as a fitness trainer a few years earlier. Fast forward to the present day and look at what a high demand there is for me, as a fitness trainer/coach.

Throughout the years, I've learned to accept the fact that I was the best version of my father; strong, powerful, and unstoppable. I also learned, to become a more loving person to myself and be the best coach, I had to reconcile with my past. Forgiveness is so liberating. I learned to forgive and love my father instead of hating him. I inherited his strong genes. And just like him, I have so much love for people, and his love for health and fitness which later in life became a very successful career choice for me. My father was a hard-working man and so am I. I made a vow to myself, never again will I speak ill of my father and I will always love him. A huge emotional burden was taken off my shoulders by reconciling with my father and my past.

At the beginning of my search to become a trainer, I felt the odds were against me because of the color of my skin and my thick accent. I went through many, many sleepless nights crying all night and ended up working in places as a trainer for low-paying positions. I poured my love and attention on my clients and they all wanted to come back. That's how I ended up getting a raise in pay.

I got a job as a trainer in a martial arts facility called Billy Blanks World Training Centre and learned martial arts, as well. Billy was a 7th-degree black belt in Tae Kwon Do. He created a style of workout, called 'Tae Bo.' I earned my black belt in Tae Kwon Do at the age of 46. I became one of his Tae Bo girls, teaching Tae Bo in his studio.

A funny story happened when Tae Bo was very popular, and the media was in a frenzy over it. One day, we were told that a film crew from a local TV station was coming to film us during the class. It was to be shown live, by the way. The line was very long to get into that class because Billy was the teacher. I was on the stage with him as his assistant. I was told the TV reporter was coming on the stage to participate. Whilst I was throwing a sidekick, the reporter suddenly jumped in front of my kick. The kick landed on his tummy. I accidentally kicked him off the stage and he fell on top of a few spectators. I was petrified, but everybody else was laughing hysterically. Needless to say, the poor guy was very embarrassed and realized he had come on the stage at the worst moment. He was the one who apologized to me.

As talented as I was in martial arts and because of my popularity, I could feel so much hatred towards me in the Tae Bo gym. I felt threatened by the possibility that I would be kicked out very soon. So, I quickly started studying Pilates and yoga and decided to expand my knowledge of fitness.

Once again, my friend, Chloe saved me and helped me get a part-time job as a yoga instructor in a very upscale gym in Los Angeles, called MARINA CITY CLUB (MCC), but only for one hour a week.

About a year later, Chloe suggested I should add another class of kickboxing right after yoga class. Then Chloe left her job in that gym. As the months went by, I noticed my hours were getting shorter and shorter at Billy's. I got very worried. I felt so insecure in that place. I feared that soon I could no longer afford to pay my rent.

After having so many sleepless nights, praying and asking for guidance, I had an a-ha moment leading me to move on to another line of fitness. Since I had become a certified Pilates instructor, I decided to purchase a Pilates Reformer, but I had no idea where to go with it and how to get clients. I just knew I had to purchase this machine. I had no money to buy it, so I charged it to my credit card, not knowing where I was going to put it at the time of delivery. It was arriving in five weeks.

I made an appointment to have a meeting with the manager of MCC and I told him I needed the vacant room in the gym to place my Pilates Reformer and start training. He approached me and stated that the members of the club didn't want me to be there as a full-time person. Once again, I was not approved because of my nationality.

This time, I approached the general manager of the entire MCC and pleaded with him to find a way for me to use that vacant room. I needed to have a job somewhere, I had so much to offer. I called him 10 times in seven days. After all, he was in charge and it was his decision. Then I made a vow to him that within the next six months, if I didn't get a few new members to join, they could get rid of me. He said he would think about it. My Reformer was arriving soon. I was worried and didn't know what to do with myself. Then one day I got a call that the Pilates machine arrived and they needed a location to deliver it .I prayed endlessly and called the manager once again. He said he was just about to call me to say I was approved and I could start using that vacant room to teach Pilates.

Within six months I recruited 10 people to become members of the club and my career and reputation began to soar.

To this day, every NO I've gotten, I've turned it into a big fat YES!

I will never give up.

I was put on this earth, to love to help to share and lift others, and to be an example of perseverance, I didn't come this far to lose hope and let the music die in me.

As long as I can remember, I have had the Almighty on my side at all times.

Fari Eskandari Gonzaque

Fari Eskandari Gonzaque holds both America and England close as her home.

With an unwavering passion for spirituality, health, and fitness, she has flourished as a successful fitness trainer and Health and Wellness coach, guiding clients on these paths for over three decades.

Through traumas and challenges faced, she has gained wisdom leading her to specialize in relationship coaching and mentoring, as well as essential self-love and self-respect.

She draws from all relationship types (work, family, romance), coupled with her own adventurous life experiences, to help clients achieve successful relationships that have otherwise eluded their grasp.

Studying from the greats, such as Ram Das, Wayne Dyer, Tony Robbins, Byron Katie, Maya Angelou, Steve Hardison, Steve Chandler, Rich Litvin, and others, she has honed her intuitive and interpersonal skills to create massive transformation in the lives of her clients.

She guides them to find the diamond in their trauma.

Fari has a deep-seated calling to help others learn and apply these lessons. She is happily married to the love of her life.

Her coaching services are available to those who continue to repeat the same mistakes and expect different results.

Fari helps individuals move from feeling lost and lonely to hopeful and rejuvenated through empowering self-love and respect, especially those suffering from imposter syndrome.

Connect with Fari at

https://www.faritransformation.com/.

CHAPTER 7
Say Yes to the Opportunity

by Jacalyn M. Price

I dedicate my chapter to my Aunt Eve, my mentor, and my best friend. No matter what challenges you face, there is always a way to overcome them.
Eve taught me this and much more.

Opportunities can come along to anyone at any time. No matter what your age is.

If you're young and at school, you are presented with opportunities. Even if it's in sports games, belonging to a group, like Girl Guides, a church group, dancing, or academic achievements.

In this chapter, I'm sharing the opportunities that have come along for myself, and for my family. By saying YES, giving my best, and visualizing the outcome, even before I start, the opportunities are abundant.

Say Yes to the opportunity and then work out how to do it.
~Sir Richard Branson

You don't realize, even when you're young, that it's the power of saying YES, the excitement of going forward, and the outcome that can happen in primary school.

We had sports activities, and a lot of us liked to play marbles. And it was great to join the boys because that was the biggest competition. In sports, we had the high jump and running.

I joined the Brownies at the Boolaroo Baptist church. It was a great activity for all the young girls. We had a lot of friendships, had camp, and learnt new skills.

In high school. Saying YES. We had a softball team which was a competition for all the schools. My Favorite position was catcher, and I could always hit a ball well, and had a lot of runs, too.

Saying YES. I started to work in pathology. at the Royal Newcastle Hospital. I worked in hematology and blood transfusion. This was a very rewarding career.

While attending tech college, I was asked if I would like to learn self-defense. YES of course. I learnt Judo. More new skills. You never know when you might need it. This came in handy many years later, when I was hit by a taxi at a pedestrian crossing. I went airborne, and out of instinct, I did a breakfall. I broke my right arm in six places but saved my body and my head. I spent four and a half months in the hospital and had a lot of rehabilitation. I have a bionic arm now, elbow replacement, pins, and plates in my shoulder and wrist. It hasn't stopped me, though.

YES, I had the opportunity to buy some acreage, 25 acres at Eagleton, but as a female back then it was very difficult to get a loan from the bank, even though I had a secure job. So I had to get a guarantor from a family member to be able to get the loan and purchase the property.

YES, for another opportunity, I had a tow truck license. A friend had a car wrecking business, so we would be called out to retrieve vehicles.

On the farm, we purchase young ones poultry and bring them home. We had a large open enclosure so we could fit a large number of hens, those that were old enough to lay, as well as roosters. We would collect the eggs and I would take them to work to sell at the hospital, and to local people.

And YES, to the opportunity of having some cattle. We had some Black Angus and some Herefords. Of course, they were pets as they all had names. We would collect day-old bread from Woolies to feed them. We'd purchase hay, as well.

We own our own cattle crush to be able to give them injections and check them out. We had our own cattle truck to transport, and I had my class 3 license for the five-ton truck we had on the farm.

For the eggs, we had our incubator made from an old fridge with racks to put the eggs in and lower racks for when the eggs were ready to hatch. We rotated the shelves daily and then watched as the chickens made their way out of the eggs. Once hatched, they were placed in a long timber box with a light to keep the chickens warm, and to grow enough to let in with the older chickens.

YES, to hives of bees. Being an Apiarist. I was buying honey and they said, "Why don't you have your own hives?" So, we started with a few hives, and in the end, we had 100 of them. The bees were fascinating to watch. We had our extracting van, and once we collected the frames of honey, using a hot knife, took the top layer off the frame. We would then spin the honey out, then bottle it. We call it Eagleton Honey. We would sell honey locally and take it to work as well.

I traveled to Gatton College once for a course in Queensland, on artificial insemination of the queen bee. Very interesting. We met a lot of other beekeepers there. One of the couples we met while we were at that college in Queensland, Thelma and Charlie, they had a property on North Stradbroke Island. We were invited to visit them. So we did, we went across on the ferry to North Stradbroke Island.

YES, I worked as an Avon representative. I was in the top 50 in Australia for sales. One year, I won the Mrs. Albee award and a seven-night cruise around the islands off of Queensland—an adventure of a lifetime.

I started learning ceramics. It was very rewarding. Bev was my teacher. We made anything from clocks, fruit bowls, plates, animals, birds, and more. And I was invited to do a teaching course. I said YES. I, along with many others accepted and completed the course.

While on holidays, YES, we traveled to Western Australia, and visited all the places, and one of them was Monkey Mia. I had the opportunity to feed the dolphins. We would enter the water and hold the fish up ready for the dolphins who would come along and take it out of our hands—an amazing experience, and everyone enjoyed it. It was a beautiful location with lots of birds, and just being in the water with the dolphins. It was so rewarding.

While on holidays, YES, we chose to go to Tasmania and took the motor home on the ferry across on the Spirit of Tasmania. It's an overnight trip. We spent a month in Tasmania, visiting all the sites, and traveling all around Tasmania. We visited Cradle Mountain, camped in the Parks had local animals visit us at Lake St. Sinclair National Park.

You never know. Life can change in a split second.

A Simple fall at work many years ago left me unable to work for many years. There were a lot of rehabilitation pain clinics, I spent a lot of time using a wheelchair, mobility scooters, a walking frame, and crutches.

I entered a competition and won $5000 in travel.

So, YES, I decided to use this to go to England. My dad had a half-sister, Ivy, in Smithwick in England. Dad's parents came from England. His mum was from

York and his dad was from Birmingham in the town of Smithwick. We stayed there for a month, we took her to London and went on a cruise down the River Thames. We stayed in a motel there and what an experience for Ivy, she never forgot.

We visited Buckingham Palace and saw the changing of the guards. We visited Windsor Castle and took minibus tours all around England. We went through the Channel Tunnel to Paris on the Eurostar, the bullet train.

We stayed in Paris for a few days, visited the Eiffel Tower, and saw the amazing view from the top. We went for a cruise down the River Seine and saw a lot of historic landmarks. We also saw the follies dances, an amazing experience.

All of this was also done while I was using my walking frame and it had crutches attached to it. It doesn't matter what problem you have, you can go anywhere you like, and still enjoy yourself.

With the rest of the money I won, we took a trip to New Zealand. Dad's parents had a successful business in New Zealand in the 1920s. A lorry and truck business in the horse and cart era. Of course, in New Zealand, there were always lots of earthquakes. The buildings were built so that they would sway gently when the earthquakes came to avoid collapse. My uncle would tell me that as a child in New Zealand, they would watch the buildings sway and be amazed at how they just swayed and stayed up.

My grandfather, James Samuel Price, also built a special wall near their home so if there were any problems with earthquakes, the earth wouldn't come down and damage the business. When we went over there, he showed me the wall and showed me the home where his parents lived, the school he attended, and where he spent his childhood until the Depression hit. Then my grandfather lost his business and had to come back to Australia.

My grandfather used to live in Wellington, New Zealand, and when we made a trip back there, we visited Wellington and went on city tours. We went on the cable car to Wellington with amazing views from the heart of the city up through the hillside, terrace houses of Kilburn, to the lookout perched above the city.

We traveled by car and looked at the sights while we were on the North Island, toured a car museum as well, and looked at the cars my grandfather had.

I also went on a helicopter ride to Mount Cook, landed in the snow, and went for a walk. The first time I had been in snow, an absolutely amazing experience.

Another YES was an opportunity to take my mum, dad, and aunt on a two-night cruise from Newcastle to Brisbane. We sailed on the Pacific Sun. Mum and Dad and my aunt had never been on a cruise before. And it was a lifelong dream to do so.

They had the trip of a lifetime eating, exploring the ship, and buying souvenirs, there was plenty to eat and hot spas. Dad fell out of bed the first night. Luckily, he was on the lower bunk. We laughed so much trying to get him back into bed but there was no injury.

And we went down to the Gold Coast to see sights.

We took Mom and Dad on a helicopter flight. I had never been on a helicopter flight before, and I loved it.

Another YES. I had more holidays.

We drove to Darwin from Newcastle, a trip of over 3800 kilometers. We had a lot of stops along the way visiting the sites. Kakadu National Park, Ayers Rock, back then we could climb up to a certain point using a chain. We couldn't climb the whole way up anymore. Then we walked around the rest, which is quite a distance, but it was just an amazing place.

We visited the Devil's Marbles and Kings Canyon, we walked all around the base of the canyon. And the sights from the bottom to the top of the canyon are amazing.

We visited the Katherine Gorge and had a trip along the gorge, and we visited Mataranka hot springs or thermal pools—very invigorating.

Another YES, while on holidays, I drove to Cairns, visited the Great Barrier Reef, and went snorkeling on the reef.

We also had glass bottom boat tours, just watching all the fish swimming on the reef and the colours of the reef and all the fish while in the area. We went on the Kuranda scenic railway, went to Daintree Forest, and to Port Douglas.

While doing a network marketing course, I was offered to go to the next stage. Of course, I said YES. I flew to the United States and went over to Miami, Fort Lauderdale.

We then went on a 10-day cruise marketing cruise. While at sea, we had a networking event, listening to the experts—authors. While in port, we visited all the small islands. We had a trip to Mexico as well.

We visited the local areas while in Miami. We went on a trip into the Everglades, watching the alligators, one nursing a baby alligator at the zoo. The Cruise was

"Markets Gone Wild." I met Robert Allen, an author and a successful business owner, as well as many other business owners.

We visited Las Vegas and stayed at the Circus Circus Hotel. I watched a circus show at night. We visited another hotel where we had white lions coming in each day.

While in San Francisco, I visited Alcatraz Island. It was unreal to just walk through that place and see what went on back then. We viewed all the sites, and went to the Golden Gate Bridge, on an open-top bus. And what you can see from that open top it's amazing.

YES, during a networking course, I was offered the opportunity to travel to Thailand. We had a group of us travel there. We took a cruise down the river. So, we went from people who lived in small huts on the river to going to the far end, where there was a mansion of gold, one extreme to the other. Yet, all those who lived on the river were very happy.

While we were attending lessons one day, we had the monks visit us and give us a blessing.

Another night we all lit Lanterns and released them into the sky. It was amazing. Watching your lanterns go skyward.

I was invited to attend a business opportunity with ACN—All Communications Networks.

Of course, I said YES. It's simple, but just not easy. Everybody pays bills. I can help the business owner and the household save on bills. I have a part-time income, as I'm a carer for my parents.

I was having some training with Matt Morris, an international speaker. And he said, "Would you like to co-author with me? Of course, I said, "YES. I've always wanted to write a book."

So, my book is *Breakthrough Leadership with Jacalyn Price*.

I'm on the front cover with Matt Morris, and there are 29 other leading experts in the book, as well. This was my first start with a book and has led to many more books.

I joined an author's group, of course, I said YES. So, with Lynda Sunshine West and Sally Green, I am co-authoring other books. The first one is *Action Takers Who Get Shit Done-No Excuses* and *Never Give Up*. and the next book, just about to go in, is *Unstoppable Female Entrepreneurs*.

While at an event with the author's group, there were two prizes to be won. I won a ticket to the Prosperity Camp in San Diego, California, in January 2024.

It's amazing, synchronicity.

You never know where this will take you. saying YES.

I was also invited to co-author with Sunil Tulsiani and Brian Tracy, based in the US. I'll be on the front cover with these two legends, and I'm part of the book with other leading experts, as well. This is another exciting chapter I'll be writing.

Sunil offered some books to purchase, some he had written and coauthored, and another YES, I have seven more books to my collection. I also have a special gold coin, which says, *I am a money magnet, and I am a multimillionaire.* Which I carry in my pocket everywhere.

As well as a gold note, where you write when you're a millionaire, I have my date on it, and it is framed and, in my study, to look at all the time.

Opportunities to say YES ... attending other networking groups, invited to be a host, co-host, and speaker at those events, building relationships and supporting each other in business.

I was asked by Peter Sage to do a course, Ultimate Self Mastery, another YES. I have just about completed this.

Eric Worre, a networking professional, was coming to Australia, another YES to attend his event on the Gold Coast, with many others.

Chuck Norris, (Walker Texas Ranger) was coming to Australia, in Sydney, another YES to see Chuck in person, with hundreds of others, many photo opportunities, a lovely man.

One time I saw an ad to join a networking group so I turned up in business attire. The first time I'd been to a live event, and I really enjoyed meeting new business owners while I was there. The owner, Matt said, "Why don't you put an application in for the awards coming up soon?" So I did, of course. I made the finals and also, I was Business of the Year for business services for ACN for 2020 and 2021.

YES, to other networking groups, I have been invited to speak at events and had a 25-minute speaking spot at one time.

Saying YES to attending "Unleash the Power Within," with Tony Robbins, a 4-day event.

Doing the Firewalk twice now. I was a crew member this year as well.

I was asked if I would like to do a three-day course, "Grow Your Coaching Biz," with Sharon Jurd. Another YES. I now have my certificate, exciting.

Guess who is coming to Australia in December, Sir Richard Branson, YES, I have my ticket to go to the event.

Saying YES to the opportunity to invest in other streams of income. Attending training and learning new skills.

With Neumi. The importance of Glutathione for your body, health benefits, mental clarity, and energy.

Enagic, Kangen water. The best water available for hydrating the body as well as controlling acidosis, lasting health begins with clean intestines, increases energy, promotes good digestion, high in antioxidants, neutralizes free radicals, and returns the body to a healthy alkaline state. Detoxifies internal organs. Change your water, change your life.

Imagine saying YES to any opportunity that comes along, where it can take you.

Change your story, change your life.
~Tony Robbins

I'm Jacalyn Price, Best-selling Author, Entrepreneur, Speaker, Coach, Mentor, Investor, and Business Owner.

She believed she could, so she did.
~R.S Grey
Everything is Energy.
~Albert Einstein

Jacalyn Price

Jacalyn Price won Business of the Year in business services for ACN in 2020, and 2021.

She has articles published in the Bx xClusive magazine and belongs to the following networking groups business at breakfast: Edward Zia networking community; Lake Macquarie women in business, more marketing ideas; Bconnected world; happy neighborhood project. She has been a host and speaker at her networking events.

She was a finalist in the Hunter Region Business Excellence Awards, Australian Small Business Champions Awards, Australian Women's Small Business Champions Awards, Local Business Awards, Australian Ladies in

Business Initiative Awards, and Bx Business xCellence Awards.

Jacalyn has an article in the Newcastle weekly, highlighting her ACN business.

Jacalyn's key to success is personal development. Some of her biggest influences are Bob Proctor, Zig Ziglar, Mary Morrissey, Jim Rohn, Tony Robbins, Grant Cardone, Simon Sinek, and Peter Sage, to name a few.

Her mission is to set up a future foundation for people with illnesses to access funding for medication and treatments. This was after her sister Jen was diagnosed with breast cancer and had to pay a large sum for radiation treatment.

Jacalyn loves taking the burdens off families, touching hearts, and changing lives. Every day for her is a new day, with new thoughts, strengths, and possibilities.

Connect with Jaclyn at www.jacalynp.acnibo.com.

CHAPTER 8

From Setbacks to Success: Lessons in Entrepreneurship and Resilience

by Julie Page

I offer this dedication to my beloved family: Adam, Katrina, and Danielle. Their unwavering belief, constant encouragement, and countless hours of hard work were the essential ingredients that transformed my dreams into reality.

Moving from Australia to the USA, I never anticipated the immense strain it would place on my marriage and my family. My husband, originally from Australia, grappled with the culture shock and found himself starting his plumbing career from scratch – a daunting setback. This plunged us into a whirlwind of financial pressure, and we had our hands full with our two little girls, who happened to be the sweetest twins you can imagine.

Now, let's rewind a bit. I'm American, and our love story has a bit of a twist. I met my husband during my travels with a mission organization aboard a ship. We journeyed to various corners of the world, working with churches and carrying a cargo hold brimming with literature. Our paths crossed at a church gathering, where I was initially on a mission to recruit him as a volunteer for the ship ministry, while he was secretly plotting to recruit me as his life partner. Lucky for him, he won me over in the end!

After tying the knot, we made Australia our home for a decade. It became home to me. When we felt that God was leading us elsewhere, leaving behind our cherished friends and life in Australia was heart-wrenching. We sold all our possessions, condensed our lives into a few precious belongings, and embarked on a journey to start anew in Minnesota.

Our initial days in Minnesota were far from smooth sailing. As I mentioned, one of our most daunting challenges was my husband's career taking a massive step back. To add to our financial woes, we lost a hefty sum of around $50,000 due to unfavorable exchange rates at the time.

In the throes of severe stress, I've developed a coping mechanism – emotional eating. Can you relate? Whether it is financial or emotional turmoil, I reach for the chocolate to provide solace. I suppose we all have our coping mechanisms, and for me, it's a delicious escape from life's hardships.

This continued for two years until one day when I was shocked at the number on the scale! 199! That was my breaking point. I was determined NOT to be over 200 pounds. So, I began the search for a program to help me. It was called "Live It!" and it was more than just a food and exercise plan. It also incorporated beliefs and mindset. That was so important to me because I knew I had to change my thinking before I could change my habits. Shedding that weight and keeping it off, I decided that I wanted to empower and equip others to transform their health through lasting lifestyle change.

In 2002, I started in my living room with six women who wanted to better their lives through healthier daily choices. Those six women turned into over 1,500 individuals who were impacted by Total Wellness Coaching over 15 years.

So, how did I get from six to 1,500? Well, it was not without a lot of time, challenges, and hard work. I have often heard it said that "if being an entrepreneur were easy, everyone would be doing it." But I will say that I thought it would be a little easier! In this chapter I want to share a few lessons that I learned along the way, in hopes that you will walk away encouraged and empowered to move forward and make a difference in your business.

I started as a sole proprietor, working out of a local gym, partnering with another Personal Trainer. Those were the sweet days of no overhead and not a whole lot of stress.

When I expanded in 2008, I opened my own personal training studio and launched my signature boot camp program, which blended the benefits of group fitness, together with personal accountability, goals, and nutrition education. I was growing and very successful. However, I dreamed of having a team one day. That day came in 2011, when I launched a group fitness program. I had employees – a team. But, of course, all dreams are not always as dreamy as we dreamed they'd be. If you have had employees, you know that they can be both a blessing and a stressor at times.

For example, an employee unilaterally canceled a fitness class, violating our no-cancellation policy. We prided ourselves on never canceling classes, valuing our members' anticipation. Our team was sizable, making it easy to find a substitute when someone was unwell.

Conflict, a necessary but challenging aspect of entrepreneurship, loomed as I contemplated firing her later that day. I felt nauseous and terrified; I had never fired anyone before. To my relief, upon returning to my office, she had left proprietary materials and her resignation letter. I was saved this time.

Another employee, hired prior to becoming a certified trainer, failed to pass the certification test after months of studying. Despite extended support, I carried her for about ten months, waiting for her to meet her end of the agreement. She did not. Her response was far from understanding or apologetic when I let her go. Instead, I received a barrage of harsh letters, emails, and texts, absolving her of responsibility. Lesson learned: I decided to hire only those already certified in their profession.

I have more stories to share, but I'll spare the details here. The most significant lesson I learned from having employees is how to care for them without attempting to rescue them. In both cases above, I was trying to assist two individuals with substantial potential, but they were unwilling to invest the effort to realize it. I believed I could do the work on their behalf, but it backfired. We can have faith in others, but we cannot infuse them with self-belief. They must desire to cultivate their own belief. I have had to learn to let go because when you desire something more for someone than they want for themselves and assume responsibility for that desire, no one emerges victorious.

A few years later, while in lease negotiations with my landlord, I received an eviction notice. The lease would not be renewed and I had six months to decide: Was I going to close down? Or take a giant leap of faith and expand again? I decided to expand.

I found a 5,000-square-foot place locally. It allowed me to have a group fitness class, a boot camp class, a spinning class, and two personal training clients all at the same time. For the first time in my ten plus years of business, I had a large loan from the bank. We had to renovate the space from an old beauty school into a fitness facility.

Making hard decisions is part of being a fearless entrepreneur. Now, I admit that I did not feel fearless at the time. I was scared to death! As Franklin D Roosevelt said, *"Courage is not the absence of fear, but rather the assessment that something else is more important than fear."* For me, it means taking that next step towards my dream, while I am afraid. That is courage to me.

In addition, I had to sign a lease with a personal guarantee for the new space. This was incredibly scary for me, knowing that I was putting my family at risk financially. But, as a woman of faith, both my husband and I prayed and decided it was the right way forward and so we proceeded. After lots of hard work, especially by my husband on the build-out of the space, we moved into our new space. It was beautiful! A grateful day indeed.

I had built a committed community with our members. So many came to help clean the space and to move in the equipment. It was their community. A place where everyone was welcome, no matter their size, their fitness level, or their injuries. Each member left every workout feeling great because they accomplished what they set out to do.

The initial excitement quickly gave way to frustration and exasperation within one week of moving into our beautiful, new space.

The first blow was the locker room's water supply. We had barely unpacked when we discovered that the water was completely non-functional. Little did we know that this seemingly innocuous problem was a manifestation of five years' worth of neglect. The building, a former beauty school, had been left dormant, allowing clumps of hair to accumulate, harden, and clog the plumbing. It was a disaster waiting to happen, and it happened to us. We had to plead with the city to come to our rescue, which they did and remedied the situation in a timely manner.

And then there were the electrical issues, which added insult to injury. In the women's locker room, I had the foresight to have multiple outlets installed, envisioning a bustling hub of women drying and curling their hair simultaneously. This was communicated to the contractors. What I didn't anticipate was the electricians' mind-boggling decision to connect all these outlets to a single breaker. When I dared to question this decision, their response was nothing short of incredulous: "You didn't explicitly ask for separate breakers for each outlet. It'll cost you an extra $200 to fix." In my naivety, I assumed that the experts I hired would, well, be the experts. I never imagined that I'd have to moonlight as an electrician. The sigh that escaped me was laden with a profound sense of exasperation, carrying the weight of all the vexation and bewilderment that had transpired in a mere week.

After the first few weeks of working out kinks, however, our new place was a dream come true. Unfortunately, that dream only lasted about two years.

In 2017, I had a car accident. A woman hit me while she was driving backwards down the street. Yes, you heard me right – backwards! Who looks for vehicles driving backwards before you turn? Well, now I do! At that same time, I had built my business to be a well-oiled machine. I had two full-time personal trainers besides myself. I had a full class schedule with happy, healthy members. Things were good. I was happy to continue until I retired. But, due to the injuries from the car accident and an offer to buy the fitness studios, I decided to sell, even though it was for less than what the business was worth at the time. I was ready to hand over the success to another and launch a new adventure.

After spending several years in management, I embarked on an exciting new journey by establishing my own venture, IMPACT Coaching Solutions. Drawing upon the invaluable insights I've gained during my experiences, I've channeled those lessons into the growth of my coaching, speaking, and training business. My commitment to personal and professional development led me to become a Maxwell Leadership Certified Team Member, ensuring that my own growth continues to benefit and empower others.

What truly fuels my passion is witnessing the transformative "aha" moments experienced by my coaching clients. These moments mark the breakthroughs they've longed for but struggled to achieve independently due to feeling utterly stuck. Moreover, I take immense delight in seeing teams conquer hurdles by fostering effective communication that unites them and catalyzes greater collaboration. My purpose, my very joy, lies in the empowerment and equipping of individuals like you to unearth your hidden potential and realize your dreams.

Essential takeaways from my journey:

1. **Get out of your way!** When I first started my business, I took any client, as long as they were breathing! I did not do a good job of asking questions to ensure the client was ready to make lifestyle changes. This led to a lot of "D" clients, rather than "A" or "B" clients. A "D" client is someone who would not complete their action steps between training sessions, or who would just not show up for their training.

First rule, if you want to be successful in business, is to stop thinking about yourself, and think about what the client needs. Listen. Ask questions. For example, rather than worrying about "can I charge that amount?"

or "who would want to hire me?" or "I don't know what I am doing!," listen. Ask yourself while you are listening, "can I help them?" or "do I have the tools and skills that can help them on their journey?" or "how can I serve them?"

My first coach put things into perspective for me. I was at the very beginning of my business journey and I was so worried about what others thought of me – any other people pleasers out there? You know what I mean! Well, I almost fell off my chair when she said, "Julie, I am so sorry to burst your bubble, but NO ONE is thinking about you! In fact, everyone is so focused on their own selves, they don't give a single thought about you." Well, at first I was a little like, "How dare you?," but then I realized she spoke the truth. I will always be grateful to my first coach who helped me to get out of my own way so I could move forward in success.

2. **Stop taking things personally!** This really piggybacks on point number 1, and is another area that I have had to grow a lot in.

One of my first personal training clients helped me grow in this area. She was so direct and blunt, that my sensitive self would come away hurt and thinking she did not like me. That would cause me to shrink when in her presence, which meant I was not doing my job of training her as she was paying me to do. She helped me build backbone and a little toughness, which I will always be grateful to her for.

> For example, our first training sessions were something like this.
>
> Client "I don't want to do that exercise."
>
> Me "Umm. Ok. Would you like to do this instead?"
>
> Client {Swear words}
>
> Me – {Giving into Client}
>
> After growth example:
>
> Client "I don't want to do that exercise."
>
> Me "You told me you have a goal for stronger arms. Has that goal changed?"
>
> Client {Swear words} "Can I do bicep curls instead of push-ups?"
>
> Me "No. Get down there and give me 20 push-ups! You got this."
>
> Client {grumbling} but does the push-ups.

3. **How much you are willing to GROW will largely determine how far you will GO in your life and business.**

a. **Read.** Every successful entrepreneur is always reading. If you don't like to read, listen to books. Reading expands our horizons and challenges us to grow. My goal is to read a growth book every month. There are great authors out there who will challenge you to grow. Three of my favorite books, at this time, to get you started:

   i. *How to Win Friends & Influence People* by Dale Carnegie

   ii. *Eat That Frog!* by Brian Tracy

   iii. *The 15 Invaluable Laws of Growth* by John C. Maxwell

b. **Hire a Coach.** I understand that this is an investment in you, which is hard to do mentally, as well as financially, when an entrepreneur. However, I guarantee it will be the best investment you ever make in yourself personally and professionally. It is important to choose wisely. I have had great coaches and not-so-great coaches in the past. Things to look for in a great coach:

   i. **You want to feel a connection** with them.

ii. **You want to experience** a coaching session with them before signing an agreement. Great coaches offer a free coaching session (not a consultation) where you will walk away with action steps to implement.

iii. **A great coach asks great questions**, empowering and equipping you to break through obstacles, uncover new opportunities, and move faster towards the results you deserve.

I still use the lessons I learned from my executive business coaches 15 years ago. And I treasure and appreciate my current coach. He has challenged me, stretched me, and encouraged me. Me, and my business, are better because of my coaches over the years.

c. **Network with Like-Minded Entrepreneurs.** Being an entrepreneur is hard. So, embrace the difficulties by building relationships that are supportive and encouraging. You will want to have three groups of people in your network.

i. **Those who are in front of you.** You want people who are more successful than you so that you can ask questions and learn from them. As John C Maxwell says, "If you are at the head of the class, you are in the wrong class!"

ii. **Those who are walking alongside you.** You want people who can walk with you, support you, and understand your current challenges. Just make sure that they are positive people who will speak truth and encourage you to keep moving, rather than people who will sit and have a "pity party" with you.

iii. **Those who are behind you.** You want people who you can add value to. People who you can help because you have already walked in their shoes.

d. **Be consistent in your daily disciplines.** Learn a little; do a little. Consistent action daily toward your goals is the key. My two favorite quotes are:

   i. *"Every action you take is a vote for the person you want to become."* James Clear

> *ii. "The secret of your success is determined by your daily agenda."*
> John C Maxwell

4. **Be willing to make the hard decisions.** Stand firm on your values, vision, and mission. It is your business, your reputation. Others will not always understand. And in fact, many people do not take responsibility for their own action or inaction. Rather, they will play the blame game or play the victim. Stand firm!

I have found having a best friend who can listen objectively and give wise counsel, even though she is not a business owner, has been invaluable to me. My supportive business network and my coach have also been of great value in these difficult times. It is so easy for me to be too sensitive or let my emotions show in these situations. Having the support, encouragement, and wise counsel from "my people" has saved me more than once.

My parting words of wisdom: Never, ever surrender. Embrace setbacks as springboards for comebacks. Accept your failures; they're part of the learning journey. Laugh at yourself, a lot. Invest in your personal growth daily and consistently. Keep moving forward, even when trembling. Establish healthy work-life boundaries. And, above all, know you're not alone; you're living your purpose! You've got this!

Julie Page

With over two decades of experience as a successful business owner and life coach, most of which was in the fitness and wellness industry, Julie Page has a passion to create business teams where employees thrive, both personally and professionally.

As a Maxwell Leadership Certified Team Member, specializing in Speaking, Coaching, and Training, she works alongside organizations to improve effective and clear communication amongst team members, leading to elevated morale, higher retention rates, and increased profitability for the organization.

Having ventured to more than 50 countries worldwide, she offers a unique and diverse global perspective shaped by her own experiences, including those lessons gained the hard way. Her ability to share these engaging stories will keep your team captivated and entertained while imparting invaluable lessons for personal and professional growth.

By employing insightful coaching techniques and time-tested processes, Julie delves deep within organizations to unearth the root causes of challenges hindering employee advancement in leadership and job performance.

Are your team members stuck, rather than unstoppable? Develop greater collaboration, energy-giving teamwork, and clear communication, making your work culture desirable and an unstoppable force in your industry. Contact Julie today to move from Stuck to Unstoppable in your business.

Connect with Julie at https://www.impactcoach4u.com.

CHAPTER 9
Mission First, People Always

by Kathi Sohn

This chapter is dedicated to my late husband and soulmate, David William Sohn. His love, wisdom, and vision continue to inspire me every day.

I don't remember a time in my life when I wasn't on a mission. I suppose I had brief moments of languor in my crib when there wasn't some force driving my activities. From ambitious dreams in childhood to my thirty-six years in United States Defense, and into my current work to help break the cycle of generational trauma, I have continually been a woman on a mission. I have also always loved people, although I went through many years afraid to talk to them. Through much personal growth, I've overcome those fears and now, as an entrepreneur, I think of my work as a mission, not just a business. It drives me out of my comfort zone every day as I keep increasing my capacity to reach more people with my message and my work.

If I were to take a time machine to visit my younger self, I would observe some experiences and personality traits that definitely helped bring me to this entrepreneurial point in my life. I'd see myself running the little stand at the end of our driveway, selling vegetables from our garden to passersby. The scene would shift and I'd hear myself explain to my mother an idea I had for an invention. I used to find a light bulb, then run into the room holding it over my head, excitedly yelling, "I've got another great idea!" I'd also hear some remarks from my dad that helped me greatly, while also nearly preventing me from going into business for myself.

My father and mother were young children during the Great Depression and like many in their generation, they had a very practical approach to income and financial security. Dad worked for a Navy contractor most of his life. I remember him telling me, more than once, how important it was to find a job I could stick with for many, many years, and then I'd be well set up for retirement. As it turned out, I exceeded his conservative choice of employment by working not for a private company, but for the federal government for over 36 years.

I consider myself very lucky to have had such an exciting Defense Department career, but there was a price I paid for being committed to working for someone else all those years. I was never bored, traveled, worked in three war zones, and always had a lot of latitude to choose the most challenging and sometimes dangerous assignments. On the one hand, I gained much knowledge and many skills and abilities to tackle anything I'd one day face as an entrepreneur. On the other hand, I operated under layers of bureaucracy and it was difficult to create much-needed change. Always challenged to be a "self-starter" and an "independent thinker," I'd present brilliant, well-thought-out ideas (without the light bulb) to my superiors and then have to wait for 28 signatures and *possible* funding for the project in the following fiscal year. I was told I couldn't talk to the media (there was a division that did that) and as the defense budget continually dwindled after 9/11, one had to wait for several years for even the most deserving of promotions.

It was near the end of my career, with retirement in sight, that something happened that prompted my almost immediate retirement from the federal government. In late 2019, My husband of twenty-two years died. I was left in a personal crisis just before the impending COVID-19 global pandemic. I suddenly found myself a widow and single mom of two young children, on assignment in the expensive state of Hawaii. The schools shut down because of COVID, so I needed to pay hundreds of dollars every week for childcare while I continued to work until my retirement at the end of that school year.

Fifteen months after losing David, I retired and mostly settled into my new home in Alabama. The kids and I were adjusting to the "new normal" and I had decided to continue David's work, the Body Memory Process. David had created the process to help liberate people from the self-limiting and sometimes self-destructive beliefs they made up in early childhood. David's unique, powerful method of discovery and release of what he termed "childhood vows." He had served hundreds of clients for over 30 years, mostly before the Internet, and he loved empowering people.

The Body Memory Process is based on three main research-backed tenets: the power of beliefs to shape our reality, the mind-body connection, and the creative awareness of babies in the womb, at birth, and during early childhood. The pre-logical leaps children make about themselves, others, and life, based on observations and experiences they don't understand, are traumatic. These beliefs are self-fulfilling prophecies that can be limiting and even destructive as they are carried into adulthood. They are often the reason people end up ill, lonely, and broke. Well-meaning parents can be unaware of how damaging their words and actions can be, and they likely still carry their unhealed trauma from their own childhoods.

When he passed, my husband left me a legacy full of potential for helping a world ever-increasingly in need of trauma healing, the courage to dream again, and a way to realize those dreams. Then, with my newly found time in retirement and the power of the Internet, I knew that I had it in me to take the Body Memory Process, reach more people with the work, and do a lot of good in this world.

When David and I met, he was just beginning to work on his book about the Body Memory Process. I loved to write and edit, so I offered my editing services and that was the beginning of what would be 25 years of learning and experiencing the work at a very deep level. It was the Body Memory Process that helped me discover the root cause of what had been an extreme, lifelong, fear of speaking to groups. The result was complete relief from gripping anxiety and now public speaking is an easy and very fulfilling part of my work. I still come up against frontiers as I speak to larger, different audiences. But I am now able to move through and not be paralyzed by the fear. So, it was not only my love for David and my belief in how powerful the work can be in people's lives, but my own transformation that has now made this work my new mission.

Another reason it was easy for me to take on the Body Memory Process mission was what I had witnessed as a graduate student in conflict analysis and resolution. Twenty years ago, while conducting my thesis research in the war-torn city of Vukovar, Croatia, I met people who were traumatized by the Balkan war that had ensued during the breakup of the former Yugoslavia. They were also traumatized by wars they had not lived through but felt they had because of stories from their parents and grandparents. This transgenerational transmission of trauma was certain to continue with the children of the most recent Balkan war, through symbols and the continued oral tradition of their ancestors—the rhetoric of hatred.

If people do not work on themselves to become self-aware of destructive beliefs, heal their childhood trauma, and empower themselves, the cycle of trauma continues in the family, in society, and on a global level. It is the cause of domestic violence, drug addiction, criminal behavior, suicide, mental illness, and conflict on every scale.

In the first year of building the business, I spent most of my time working on a course to teach the Body Memory Process and learning how to market online. By the end of the year, I was disappointed that I had made no course sales and while I had lots of "thumbs up" on my advertising, it didn't create any leads. It was tenacity that fueled my creative problem-solving and an attitude that nothing was going to be a roadblock to the changes I needed to make in my strategy. So, I pivoted the following year to embracing the media I had been told most of my life to stay away from. It was clear that someone looking at an ad for three seconds was not going to kindle a desire for personal change, but listening to a podcast interview or reading a story just might.

I was not prepared for the incredible metamorphosis that I experienced by allowing myself to be interviewed on podcasts! It began with my preparing multiple talking points, which I soon found to be more of a hindrance than help. After about the fifth podcast interview, I finally decided to ditch the notes. As I became increasingly more comfortable in front of the camera, I began creating my own videos and eventually started doing Facebook Live videos. I started getting clients, many of whom had heard me interviewed on a podcast and my confidence soared. At the same time, I began seeing myself grow as an expert and realized it was time to write my own book on the work I was doing.

My journey to being an expert included many changes, both on the inside and in my external environment. My mindset gradually shifted as I increasingly viewed myself as the new face of the business, which I had once supported entirely behind the scenes. I hired a mentor for public speaking and expert positioning, learned how to market my newly published book, and polished off my transformation with the realization that I wanted to be a parent coach.

Because the Body Memory Process could help people of all ages with all kinds of problems, it had always been a marketing challenge to target a niche. When I decided to become a parent coach to help empower moms and dads, both personally and as parents, to ultimately empower their children, I knew that I had truly made David's work my own. I have also begun referral networking in my local area, which helps me remember that while my mission is first, people are always what matters most.

In conclusion, I have four recommendations for anyone wanting to be unstoppable in their business and in life:

1. Always be in integrity—Be honest with yourself first and others, always. It is incredibly freeing to tell the truth and accept accountability, no matter what the consequences. This always puts you in the driver's seat and you can't be manipulated by people or circumstances. Turbulent changes can happen in your business, but you'll stand strong, grounded in the truth of who you are.

2. Don't get bogged down in events and issues—People underestimate the importance of keeping their level of vibration high and don't realize how they can get pulled down by the appearance of failure or what's happening in the world around them. It's good to stay informed about events and involved in issues if you have something to contribute. What doesn't work well is to get caught up in illusion and fear, which robs you of your ability to move ahead and make a difference.

3. Think of your business, or whatever you do for a living, as a mission in life that is fueled by your values—For example, if you value a

world where children can safely learn and grow, then any work you do to create peace, security, education, wellness, and understanding will be your mission. You will be driven by your passion to be as successful in your work as possible.

4. Take time to play—Having a mission doesn't mean always being serious and busy! Take time to play every day with children, animals, friends, and family. Play relieves stress and is like water to a thirsty plant. It will keep your imagination stoked and your heart open. So many ways we play help ground us—literally, as we run or roll or sit on the ground or floor to connect with the earth and refresh.

Kathi Sohn

Kathi Sohn retired in 2020 after 36 years with the Department of Defense. During this time she also studied with her late husband, David Sohn for 25 years. Based on David's work, the Body Memory Process—which helps people discover and release the self-limiting and self-destructive beliefs formed in early childhood—Kathi's work is now parent coaching, helping parents to learn to heal their own childhood trauma, parent consciously, and ultimately empower their children. She is also the author of *You Made It Up, Now Stop Believing It*.

Connect with Kathi at https://kathisohn.com/.

CHAPTER 10
Pegasus, Like a Phoenix Rising

by Mary-Frances Buckland

I was afraid to leave, as most women are. That was when my weaknesses became my strengths and being brave was my only decision that it was evident that I must leave to survive. Being mentally and verbally abused, I had no bruises, broken bones or cuts externally. My wounds were deep. During my journey, I was often reminded to not let my past DEFINE me, but to allow it to REFINE me. To all those who are suffering, that is no way to live. You are worthy of a good life; as hard as it may be to believe, it is true. I am grateful to the one friend who kicked me in the ass and would not let me give up on ME! My friend who supports me every day and is not afraid to point out when I get on my crazy train. "H" - thank you for being there and believing in me, but most of all reminding me to believe in me. For you, I thank God every day.

It was Father's Day when I realized my 20-year marriage had come to an end. We had been separated for over a year. Our children (ages 16 and 18 at that time) wanted to prepare a family breakfast for their father and me, in hopes we would be able to reconcile our relationship. This seemed important to our children, so I accepted their invitation.

I entered with no ill feelings or intentions. Shortly after arriving at his apartment, we began to argue. This had become our main form of communication. As I attempted to make my way to the door and leave, he pushed me down onto the couch and stood in my way keeping me from standing. I eventually managed to stand up after much struggle. I fled out the sliding glass door onto the back patio. Once outside, I realized our daughter was still inside. I couldn't just leave her with him. In the time it took me to turn around, he grabbed my arm and pulled me inside.

That was when the argument took a tragic turn. Before I knew it, my soon-to-be-former husband was standing in the middle of the living room. He was waving the gun and screaming. This had become a very delicate situation indeed. Sure, our marriage was over, in fact it had been for a long time.

I had never been in a situation like that before. I don't wish it on anyone. Knowing any wrong move or word spoken could be tragic, I froze with fear. I hesitated only long enough to weigh my options which were, by the way, very few. I was dealing with an irrational man with a loaded gun! He was begging for me to kill him. A cowardly request.

Why would I do that, kill him, go to jail for murder, leaving our children parentless. I would not, I could not.

Before I could react, our daughter put herself between her father and me. I will NEVER forget the words she shouted in his face, pleading with desperation for my life. "Dad, just STOP! Can't you see she doesn't love you anymore? Just let her go!" I still choke tears when these words resonate.

Thank God, the plea of a very brave 16-year-old girl broke through the raging emotions of her father, keeping her mother from being killed with his fit of rage. Blind, unconditional fit of rage.

"Please don't do this, Mary-Frances."

Those words echoed in my head as I stared back at the reflection in the mirror. The face looking back at me was void of any particular emotions; instead, more apathetic even to itself, which was surprising since it was, in fact, my wedding day (a day that was to be the happiest day of my life) and the face looking back at me was my own.

The day was Saturday, October 19, 1991. I was just 25 years old. The following is a recollection of the day as it plays out in my today-mind, some 30 years later, post-divorce from the man I married on that balmy Florida afternoon in October.

The ceremony took place in a Lutheran Church that my husband's family had been members of for many years. It was a pretty traditional wedding as far as weddings go. Nothing extraordinary had been planned; simple was good for me. My father gave me away as friends and family witnessed. My best friend was my bridesmaid, my sister my maid-of-honor, her girls were the flower girl and junior bridesmaid. My husband to be, his grooms part including his oldest son and his youngest was the ring bearer.

My dress... ahh, yes, the dress. White with puffy sleeves and a lace bodice purchased from the JC Penney catalog for a mere $125. I loved that dress. I wore a dome shaped silk hat with pearls and a veil pushed back and, on my feet, much to my mother's horror, I donned white lace granny boots that would carry me down the aisle.

There was a kind of dull, white-noise background sound as the bustle of everyone mulling around as they were engaged in preparation of the main event, everyone focusing on their assigned tasks. As I stood there, all alone, quietly looking at myself in the mirror, I carefully applied my make-up and styled my hair. Not being a big fan of fuss and muss, I chose to do it myself. My mother was minding the children to ensure they stayed relatively clean for the ceremony. My father was in and out, taking candid, behind-the-scenes pictures. I remember that he made me feel uncomfortable and embarrassed as I primped myself.

I remember thinking how odd it was, although it didn't necessarily involve any emotion to me at that moment. It was as if noticed through the eyes of an onlooker as the emotion filled words my father spoke to me that morning sitting on the side of my bed, "Please don't do this, Mary-Frances," continued to run through my mind as I prepared to walk into the sanctuary.

My soon-to-be husband was at the front of the church, surrounded by our small wedding party. Everyone was waiting for me to walk down the aisle and stand next to him. My father turned to me as he was giving me away. It was a pleading look, begging me, yet again, not to proceed with the nuptials, it was not too late to back out. I do not recall any details of what the church looked like or how it was decorated. I do, however, remember walking down the aisle. Those white lace boots did a fine job walking me down the aisle. When I finally arrived at the altar at the side of my husband-to-be, he did not comment on how beautiful I looked, as you would have expected, nor did he gaze at me with any sense of desire or even love. That was probably the first pang of dejection I felt that day, however it didn't linger.

The ceremony began and when the vows and the exchange of rings were complete, it was time to "kiss your bride." THE KISS! The kiss I received was one like you would give your grandmother. It was a weak-ass kiss, void of what one would expect on their wedding day. Not one like the hot, steamy one in the movies that

I expected. There was NO passion, Fire, excitement or even enthusiasm behind it. It was more of a quick kiss of obligation. Not one that delivered the message to me how excited he was that we would now be spending the rest of our lives together or how much he wanted me—all of me. As I look back, I believe this was a projection of what would come my way over the following 20 years of marriage to him.

On that day, I never would have imagined my marriage ending in divorce. I was, or I thought I was, forever in love. I do not wish it had never happened, nor would I do most things different. I would not have my two beautiful children or my adorable grandson and granddaughter if I had.

It was in our first year of marriage when I had the strong feeling in my heart things were not right. We had to move, and we were packing. We had a marker fight as we were labeling boxes. I remember laughing and shrieking as we chased each other around the duplex. Honestly, this was the last happy memory I have in our relationship. The "love" in my heart had worn off by then. I know now that I did not marry because I was "in love;" however, I married because I was "in lust." I didn't know the difference between the two, and that was unfortunate. I held on to "us" hoping things would work and I might make love out of nothing at all.

Looking back, reflecting on all the signs, signals, and flashing warning lights, I know I should have. I am not one to quit or give up. However, I should have.

I attempted to hide my misery from everyone in many ways. I painted a pretty smile on my face for the public to view. I refer to it now affectionately as my "paper plate smile." I tried to hide my pain in many ways; a false smile being only one. I would alienate people, not letting anyone close enough to know how I was doing emotionally. I weighed 425 pounds and used my weight as my armor or my personal cloak of invisibility, my defense mechanism (no one wants to be near a fat person). I now realize I was only hurting me; the outside showed the pain on the inside.

I planned family outings for the kids. Camping, fishing, and swimming were some of their favorites. I was unsuccessful in my husband's accompaniment on such outings. Holidays were spent begging their father to get out of bed so we could celebrate. Weekends were for him to sleep all day. Our children still hold these memories. I can only imagine their thoughts of this now. They suffered from the absence of a father living in the same house. Children growing up with two happy parents living in separate houses is healthier for them than two parents living a life of misery in the same house.

My husband's adult children (from his prior wife) lived with us. It was Easter. I had worked late the prior night and was enjoying my slumber when I was awakened. It was just after 7:00 a.m. My husband demanded I wake up so his GRANDCHILD could hunt eggs and find his surprise. HIS FUCKING GRANDCHILD!! He couldn't get up for OUR kids BUT could for his grandchild and insist I participate. That was it!

I finally conceded to the need to admit that I was no longer able to live in an emotionless marriage, so I decided to leave. Not sure how he would react, I quietly packed boxes, put them in my car and placed them in a storage unit. It amuses me to see what one can accomplish in a small house if you do not obscure the view of the television.

The day finally came for me to leave. The children and I moved to my parents' house. I didn't much care what became of him. All I cared about was the children and that I had a roof over our head. Our house went into foreclosure and with his mother's help he secured an apartment and furnished it with items from our former home. That chapter is over.

What is next?

How do you rise from the ashes?

My 20-year marriage – FAILED.

My mother passed away.

My father passed away.

I found myself at a loss. I know now that this was not a loss at all. This was my beginning! I had no idea who, or what, I was. What role do I play in my "life" movie? Up to this point, you could say I was always a spectator with an occasional walk-on roll. It was time to reinvent myself! I had always been a caregiver, a wife, a mother, an employee, and often a token on someone else's game board. I had never really lived a life for myself. I was sharing this with a mentor who asked me this question that made me ponder my life. He asked, "Could it be you do not need to be reinvented, and perhaps you just need to finally discover yourself?" That made me cry. Who had I been for my whole life? That was when my journey of self-discovery began.

I started my education to become a health, life and transformational coach. That was when healing the wounds from my past began. I wrote my first solo book, "Emotionally Scammed," sharing how not knowing the difference between some emotions, you can make a lifetime of decisions based on deception. Writing the book surfaced a plethora of overwhelming emotions, far too many for me to process alone. I worked with a fellow coaching student as well as a therapist to work through it all. (I am not done… and I will not stop fighting for ME!) I put everything in God's hands to help me on my healing path and to help others as well. It has been an incredible journey!

It was during that time as well that I had the pleasure of having my grandson for the summer. Little did I know at the time what a blessing it would be.

He was getting ready to start kindergarten. He was scarred. He was scared. We talked. Boy, we talked! He shared that he was afraid to be in "big school." Would he have friends? In talking through his fears and concerns, I found myself telling him things I needed to hear at his age. I found that in my encouraging him, I grew more confident. In me helping him, he helped heal me. We were on a generational healing journey together.

It is when I choose to hold on to paradigms (a distinct set of thought patterns or a model often handed down for generations) that have been handed down from generation to generation (family china, embossed silver, or some odd knickknacks I really don't want) that I cannot seem to discard them. That which no longer serves me, no longer needs to be held. Many times, I was held back due to restrictive thoughts and/or beliefs. In discovering this, I found the useless "junk" I was not only carrying in my proverbial backpack, but I was also passing them on to my children. Correcting my thoughts and beliefs, I released their control. Releasing the weight made my mind open to learning to think positively and better myself. I surround myself with like-minded people. I choose to leave people in the past. They were in my life for either a season or a lifetime; however, they all had a reason or a lesson.

Today I wake up each morning declaring it as a day WON! I put my feet on the floor and take my first step confidently on the knowledge I gained from yesterday. I find three things to be grateful for every morning. When I rest my head at night, I reflect on my day and find three good things that happened.

I formed my company logo and mission statement from my journey. I would like to share it with you in hopes it inspires you....

Like the sunrise, let this be a reminder each dawn is a new beginning, a new chance at life.

Let the compass be a reminder that we all will need guidance from time to time.

Like the moon and stars, when all is dark around us, may we all find the courage to shine.

As you invoke on your journey, I shower you with Peace, loving light, and many blessings.

Mary-Frances Buckland

Mary-Frances Buckland is a Transformational Health and Life Coach specializing in healing wounds from the past empowering a self-actualized future. She is also a certified Reiki therapist, hypnotherapist, a certified mastermind leader, a teacher for 18 years, beekeeper, and an ordained minister. As a public speaker, she has graced the stage at Secret Knock, a Forbes, Inc., and Entrepreneur top-rated event.

Mary-Frances' career evolved from her life experiences. The proud mother of two children, her marriage ended in divorce. Afterward, she rebounded from one relationship, a pattern that would repeat itself until she realized that the universe was giving her just what she was asking for. After the passing of her parents, Mary-Frances began her journey of self-discovery as she studied to become a health, life, and transformational coach. It was during that time she realized she needed to heal from her past before she felt confident to help others. Unraveling years of abuse and neglect required forgiveness and a deep study into real and perceived emotions. Putting everything in God's hands, her healing took her on the path to help others.

Today, Mary-Frances coaches the homeless to find value in themselves as well as self-worth. This work has been a work of God as He guided her to do His work through her.

Connect with Mary-Frances at

www.MaryFrancesBuckland.com.

CHAPTER 11
Faith, Self-Worth, and Confidence

by S. Kay McBreairty

Ryan, thank you for your unwavering belief in my abilities and for seeing me in a higher light than I see myself. My confidence continues to soar as you help me embrace my worth. Your steadfast support through the twists and turns of life leaves me "unstoppable."

Learning to live a life of fearlessness has been a journey for me. I'm not saying my goal is to never be afraid—I do want to remain human after all—as if I have a choice. Fearlessly being the operative adverb, stepping forward despite the fear makes that word come alive.

Successes in my life have not been accomplished by me alone. Spirit, my community, and my own self all contribute to whatever I do. Faith, self-worth, and confidence, in particular, have led to my "Unstoppability."

FAITH

While life decisions are mine to make, not having to make them alone has tremendous value. My faith has played a huge part in my never feeling that I make a decision alone—I include my Higher Power in my daily prayer practice. Many a time have I "Stepped out in faith," and felt very comfortable doing so—ya know that ya know, that ya know. Have you ever had that feeling? It is inspiring and equips me with courage.

For example, when I got out of the U.S. Air Force, I moved to Washington State without a job or place to live. Friends each took me in for a few days. I then discovered I had a cousin in the area who was happy to have a roommate to share the rent. Check one off the list. Then I had a headhunter reach out to me for employment in law firms. I secured a job within two weeks of being in Washington. Check two.

More than once, I found that the company I was working for lacked the level of ethics with which I was comfortable. I left without having another job lined up. Each time, I moved on to something better than I would have imagined. For instance, when working for a networking company, the leaders misled customers into purchases. Within a couple of weeks of leaving that job, the Washington State Attorney General's Office contacted me for a temporary position that rapidly turned into a permanent one.

I give credit to my living a faith-filled life to having grown up in church and having parents who set an example. In a town of 500 people with three churches, you're bound to attend one of them. We knew right from wrong by the way our parents lived their lives. It didn't hurt either that every summer I attended my uncle's Bible Camp.

SELF-WORTH

While I continually excel in my "day" job, I have always had an entrepreneurial spirit; it is at the core of my fiber. I sold stitchery, Amway, Melaleuca, jewelry, candles, cars, memberships, Pampered Chef, and insurance. And

I was good at it. I earned cruises, fine jewelry, and even cash bonuses!

Though I had won awards, I wasn't able to transition to being a full-time entrepreneur. The confidence provided for consistent action and results. But because I didn't have self-worth, I sabotaged myself.

This sabotage was driven by a feeling of worthlessness. In particular, I repeatedly recreated unhealthy relationships with men who were incapable of loving, perpetuating my feeling of not deserving love. One relationship was with a philanderer and another with a substance abuser. I came to learn how I had co-created chaos by needing to win over love that wasn't possible to be given.

Today, I see how my personal growth journey led me to see that I was loved by family and friends—and not because I had to do something to earn it.

For 10 years, I focused on healing and breaking through the things that kept me in an unhealthy mindset. Through Al-Anon, an organization for the family members of alcoholics and other drugs, I learned why I kept making unhealthy choices in relationships and ways to show myself compassion for those choices. Knowing the why led to my learning to accept my inherent worth because I exist.

When working as an employee for the State of Washington, I attended a workshop that focused on defining a life mission statement. That was a great start in a positive movement for life meaning.

Al-Anon meetings and literature helped me tremendously. The emotions it opened me up to led me to see a counselor for the next step in healing. This counselor guided me to more self-awareness, understanding, and healing. I saw her until the day she asked me, "How perfect do you think you need to be to be in a relationship?" It was her way of "kicking me out of the nest."

During a visit with a dear, wise friend, I shared how unworthy I felt and how I desired to learn its origin. He shared two perspectives that created paradigm shifts in my mind and lightened my spirit.

He said he believed my feeling of worthlessness was the devil's lie working to keep me down. He also said that the persons who most impacted my lack of self-worth would answer to God. I immediately prayed to God to have compassion on those individuals.

I decided after those 10 years of focusing on acceptance of my worth, it was time to start dating again. I met a wonderful man. While the relationship did end, I am forever grateful. He taught me that I am loveable, and he cared for me during a number of health issues. His kindness touched me immensely.

During this period of growth, some items I learned from seminars and positive mental attitude books provided valuable insights. I discovered the correlation between our self-esteem and our abundance. Once I embraced that principle, my power for earning soared. Initially, I went from earning $18 an hour to $45 an hour. Within a year, I was earning $60 an hour, then $90 then $120. It was astounding to me to consider that my dad had earned $2 a day when he was a teenager in 1930, and I was earning $2 a minute in 2005. While inflation accounted for a sizable amount of the difference, the exponential increase in my earnings, in a short period of time, I attribute to having raised my self-esteem.

During my continual pursuit of business success, I was exposed to several books that helped me heal but also helped me become unstoppable. I learned the principles of success for any endeavor as they are the same for everyone.

The book of Proverbs is a book of wisdom. Since there are 31 chapters in the book of Proverbs, each day I read the chapter that corresponds to the day of the month. The wisdom that I find particularly helpful shares with us how to be in community and treat others.

When we are in harmony, our minds are more open to opportunities that present themselves.

Let's look at some of the other books that I've learned from:

Self-Love—the Dynamic Force of Success—Learn to Love Yourself—the Secret of Happiness in Life, in Love, in Everything You Do by Robert Schuller:

Once when I challenged an impossibility thinker to become a possibility thinker, his answer provided a revelation. 'It's not worth the effort,' he said. As he spoke, I studied his eyes, the window of his soul, and knew he didn't mean it. He really meant, 'I'm not worth it ...' I went to work to build up in his mind a picture of his enormous worth as a person. Then, little by little, when he began to stop hating himself and started liking himself, he came alive. ~Robert Schuller

---

Those words by Robert Schuller helped me realize that valuing myself didn't mean I was being selfish. It helped me to take care of myself first so that I could be there for others.

Co-dependent No More by Melody Beattie: I learned to overcome the drivers for and behavior of being dependent on the chaos from unhealthy relationships. I applied this principle by recognizing chaos and not accepting anything less in a relationship than being adored.

Success! The Glenn Bland Method by Glenn Bland: Having balance across Spirituality, Finances, Education, and Recreation leads to lasting success as defined by each individual—not society. From this book, I started to value and spend time on each of the four areas—prayer and Bible study practices, budgeting for what is most important to me, continual learning, and having fun. Doing those steps contributed to feeling my inherent worth and relaxing into the belief that life can be joyous.

The Success System that Never Fails—Experience the True Riches of Life by W. Clement Stone:

Decisions without actions are worthless.
Failure can be good for you. Don't let
mental walls block you in.
~W. Clement Stone

Wow, what a mouthful from Mr. Stone. What was I to do with that, I wondered. Well, as I made a decision,

I experienced great relief—it totally informed my next steps forward. My energy was renewed instead of being tied to making the decision.

I also began to pay attention to my thoughts and discovered how they influence my emotions and beliefs. You may have heard the saying, "We don't get what we want, we get what we put energy into." Energy is action in this case.

Success Through a Positive Mental Attitude by Napoleon Hill. The book:

> *Instructs you on what to do and how to do it when it comes to tapping and using the powers of your subconscious mind ... to constructively use, neutralize, control or harmonize with your passions, emotions, instincts, tendencies, feelings, moods and habits of thought and action ... how to aim high and achieve your goals regardless of the obstacles ... you will be taught these things if you read and then apply the principles.* ~Napoleon Hill

Sound a little like Mr. Stone? Thoughts, feelings, actions. Positive thoughts do impact our attitude and ability to move forward. Certainly, we are human and not always positive. But it can be a mindset shift to notice whether we are complaining or reflecting on what we can glean from any given experience.

CONFIDENCE

Confidence is something I have always had. It led to many great opportunities.

- ➢ In the U.S. Air Force, I was promoted "below the zone" (on an early track) by qualifying among dozens of my peers and being selected by a panel of officers.
- ➢ I was the sole signature authority at an Air Force Base for automating administrative offices.
- ➢ As a paralegal in Seattle, I worked at a law firm that sent me to London for two months.
- ➢ It was also an honor to work for the Washington State Attorney General's Office.

The confidence came from knowing I could do anything with God's help. As Daddy said, "Let me tell you, little girl, don't you think you can do anything without Him, but you can do anything with Him.

However, it was self-worth and self-esteem I needed to build and learn that I already had inherent worth because I exist!

Many people feel they need to develop confidence. I've found that often follows the developing of one's self-esteem. I was a bit backward on that norm; for me, confidence came first. For others, once they know they deserve their heart's desires, they can go forward with confidence.

Know that you are also inherently worthy simply because you exist. Let's begin with some self-care to build self-esteem. Why is focusing on self-care important for our journey to seeing our value? The self-esteem boost puts us in a mindset of knowing we are deserving and worthy of our heart's desires.

I get a massage; I think, "That felt great, I'll do that again."

Then I get a mani-pedi; I think, "I could get used to this."

Then I get a facial; I realize, "I feel really good."

Then I take a walk around the lake on the path under the trees; it dawns on me, "I deserve to feel this way."

Unstoppability

The next steps on my Unstoppability journey include applying concepts from a few books I was recently introduced to:

FAITH, SELF-WORTH, AND CONFIDENCE

10x Is Easier Than 2x: How World-Class Entrepreneurs Achieve More by Doing Less by Dan Sullivan and Benjamin Hardy (not to be confused with *The 10x Rule* by Grant Cardone):

Confidence is the byproduct of past successes, more than the cause of future success. Being in the gain continually boosts your confidence by allowing you to reference your progress ... By learning more from every experience you have, you'll stop repeating needless errors. You'll never plateau as a person.
~Dan Sullivan and Benjamin Hardy

Antifragile—Things that Gain from Disorder by Nassim Nicholas Taleb: A basic premise is that challenges and the unexpected are opportunities for something better. Being anti-fragile is more of a mindset in how we respond to things that disrupt our lives. When introduced to the book, I reflected on my life events and how I had responded with the belief that something good would come from what would otherwise seem negative.

For instance: In 2001, after knee surgery I got Shingles, which in turn triggered my auto-immune system, resulting in an explosive onset of systemic Arthritis that presented as Rheumatoid. Not exaggerating, a 90-year-old woman got around better than I did. For instance, I shouldn't have been driving—I couldn't turn my head because of the stiffness in my neck, and I had to drive with the palms of my hands. I couldn't pick up a glass of water with one hand.

But I just knew there would be treatment. A co-worker said to me, "I know you're asking yourself 'Why me?'" I actually never thought that way—why not me; it happens, and God is no respecter of persons.

A positive thing that came out of the illness is I no longer take my mobility for granted. Once I did get treatment that worked and I was able to walk and use my hands normally again, I started traveling without thinking I would wait for retirement to enjoy life.

In 2010 I found myself selling cars instead of taking unemployment—Project Management contracts had dried up for some time after the 2008 crash. On the day that yet another sale was stolen from me, I walked out. It turned out that the difference between what I had been earning as a project manager and selling cars was so high that I was able to go on unemployment after all.

That didn't last long. "Out of the blue," I was contacted by Bank of America when they were seeking paralegals to respond on behalf of the Chief Executive Officer to mortgage owners losing their homes due to the crash. Not only was I not betrayed on a daily/weekly basis, but I was treated with respect and valued for my skills.

Your Journey

You can see how I am helped by living by faith, developing self-worth, continually learning from wise people, and understanding why I do what I do. If any one thing I've shared helps you along the way, this writing is more than worth my time and energy—all of which are from much care and knowledge of your inherent worth. I hope you have unshakeable confidence in your path forward, being equipped with tools and support from others. Here's to your Unstoppability!

If you or someone dear to you are on active duty in the U.S. military or "out" and want guidance for your journey, I specialize in assisting veterans with their transition from military to civilian life—both before and after discharge. I coach groups of veterans through the steps to find their purpose, define their life mission statement, set their goals, and take steps to reach their hearts' desires.

Kay McBreairty

Kay is a professional Coach and Facilitator at McBreairty—Reaching Your Potential. After working with individual clients for over two decades, she now works with groups that want to align their vocation with what matters most to them and contributes to their life mission.

As a United States Air Force veteran herself, Kay provides guidance to veterans of all military services in particular to ensure they thrive in the civilian workplace and communities when they transition from active duty. She wished the same types of services were available to her when she "got out" in relation to translating military skills and experience to the civilian job market, for instance.

Kay finds that part of being unstoppable is continuing to move forward with what we know at the time. We don't need all the answers to make progress. Kay can assist you in taking informed action and having confidence in your choices.

Connect with Kay at

www.reachingyourpotential.world.

CHAPTER 12

Finding My Roots: A Journey of Entrepreneurship

by Sophie Teixeira de Abreu

Unlike many entrepreneurs who dive head-first into their passions, my journey into entrepreneurship began on a winding road filled with self-discovery and a pinch of serendipity.

I spent my childhood growing up near Paris, the vibrant aromas of my mother's kitchen surrounding me like a soft embrace every time she prepared a meal for our family. Each dish was a symphony, a testament to the rich culture that surrounded us. These moments spent watching my mother carefully craft every dish instilled in me a deep appreciation for the art of cooking. Yet, as fate would have it, my initial entry into the entrepreneurial world had little to do with pots and pans.

After moving to Barbados with my husband and our first baby in 2011, my identity underwent a massive shift. I found myself in the unfamiliar territory of not being able to work, as the island has strict rules to protect local labor. Whereas I previously spent my days in the corporate world, working in London for Estée Lauder, I struggled with the question: Who am I without my job?

To fill this void, I decided to channel my energy into creating a children's clothing brand with a fun edge. Embarking on this adventure, I dove into sewing lessons and created a portfolio full of clothing with fluorescent stitches and artsy animal prints. However, as the dream started to shape into reality, I had a sobering realization. As much as I cherished this new venture, it wasn't my true calling. Practically speaking, breaking into a market dominated by giants like Zara felt like an immense challenge. With little to no competitive advantage, I knew I had to let go.

It's often said that failure paves the way for success. While nursing the wounds of my first entrepreneurial failure, I found peace in an age-old love: cooking. I was constantly inventing new dishes for dinners with friends and family. In parallel, I joined the board of Slow Food Barbados to build educational school gardens all over the island, and my love for teaching the importance of healthy food became rooted in those years. Suddenly, the path ahead became clear. My heart, it seemed, was always destined for the culinary world, long before I even realized it.

2017 marked the year of change–although my challenges were far from over. As a family, we decided to move to Miami, and the promise of new opportunities initially masked the troubles that lay ahead. The year that followed was, without a doubt, the most challenging phase of my life.

There I was, thrown into the deep end in a city that didn't quite yet feel like home. During this time, my husband was commuting between Barbados and Miami, so I stepped up to take over most of the responsibilities at home. I also invested in a condo market and poolside restaurant in the heart of South Beach while my children were starting the year at a new school. I struggled with the cultural shifts, trying to bear the weight of managing a restaurant that was open seven days a week and demanded relentless attention. It seemed like everything that could go wrong did: air conditioners breaking down, employees not showing up for their shifts, plumbing catastrophes first thing on Saturday morning, you name it. I was completely overwhelmed physically, mentally, and emotionally. The clock seemed to run at its own pace, with days blurring into nights. It felt like there just weren't enough hours in the day to get everything done.

As the months rolled on, the strain became harder and harder to ignore. I was a shadow of my former self–irritated, exhausted, and on the brink of despair. Simple joys, like spending quality time with my kids, became strained, with my patience wearing thin. Depression took hold, and I no longer recognized myself. The migraines were a daily ordeal. I thought it was normal to take aspirin on a daily basis just to make it through the day. My sleep was absolutely horrible–I had difficulties falling asleep, and my anxieties would often wake me up in the middle of the night, leaving me tossing and turning for hours on end. I never felt truly rested, relying on a daily cup of coffee or three just to keep me going.

One of the most heart-wrenching blows came when I noticed clumps of my hair falling out. As a woman, this was terrifying for me. It quickly became frail and brittle, and I had no choice but to say goodbye to my long hair. It was a visible manifestation of the internal turmoil I was dealing with. Eventually, all of these health issues culminated in a diagnosis of subclinical hypothyroidism. On the one hand, this provided me with an answer to my declining health; on the other, it was a stark reminder of the toll this stress had taken on me.

In those moments of despair, all I wanted was to feel like my old self again. I missed that spark, that zest for life that once fueled me. I dreamed of waking up ready to start the day full of energy. I knew it was time to reclaim my life and rediscover the positivity and light that had once defined me. I was determined to heal myself from within and find my way back to a life filled with passion and purpose. The journey to recovery and rediscovery had just begun.

I soon met two different women who had gone through training at the Institute for Integrative Nutrition, and it dawned on me that this was what I was meant to do with my life. I got on the phone with the head of admissions and enrolled straight away, ready to start my training in September 2018. I was 37 and my life and health were about to take a new direction.

As I began to implement what I learned, my health improved significantly–in just three months I felt like a whole new me. I started incorporating more whole foods into my diet, more greens and raw foods, and I managed to kick my caffeine addiction with a delicious, toasted rice green tea in the morning and a mushroom "coffee" in the afternoon. Slowly but surely, I created new healthy habits that raised my energy levels naturally. Because I wasn't relying on coffee to keep me awake, I no longer had jittery nerves keeping me up at night. I focused on my water and electrolyte intake and soon, my migraines melted away, along with most of my symptoms. It was hard to believe food, one of the things I've always been most passionate about in life, is what helped me finally reconnect with my body.

I knew that I couldn't keep this information to myself, and I had to share it with my community. I wanted to help others, and women, in particular, approach food in terms of what will energize them and nourish their bodies as opposed to what will take a toll on their health. Although I didn't quite know where this journey would take me, I had faith that I would be changing people's lives for the better. I let my intuition guide me, and I quickly got to work.

At the time, I was listening to The GOOP Podcast by Gwyneth Paltrow quite a bit and was inspired not only by the content but also by the name. I wanted something similar–short and sweet–for my brand, and it just so happens that my husband's initials are RT, and he's the person with whom I feel most grounded. Thus, right before Christmas, ROOT Mindful Nutrition was born.

Empowerment through nutrition—that was, and still is, my mission. While health is the goal, I've always believed that the journey there needn't be lacking in pleasure. The vibrant flavors and comforting textures of food along with the sheer joy of eating are innate to our human experience. Yet, for so many people, this pleasure is often hindered by the weight of dietary frustrations. So, I created ROOT Mindful Nutrition as a way to help people realize that they can indulge in meals that are as equally delicious as they are nutritious and that nurture both the body and soul.

I love playing with food, marrying diverse ingredients, and breathing life into dishes that captivate the eye and seduce the palate. But my entrepreneurial journey wasn't without challenges. Back in 2019, before Covid, I was just starting my career as a freshly certified nutrition and health coach. Zoom was also a fairly recent tool in our lives, and a friend of mine challenged me to do my first cooking class online. Like most emerging entrepreneurs, I had to force myself to get out of my comfort zone and start reaching out to more people, so I accepted the challenge. That day, I posted an invitation on Instagram. There was no turning back! I was into raw food at the time, so that was the theme of my first cooking class.

There I was, teaching nine women how to make raw collard wraps. Needless to say, I knew most of those ladies, some of them friends of friends. My mother-in-law and her best friend, who are both French, were also a part of the class. Because I was doing this class in English, I had to translate most of it for them, which turned the whole thing into joyful chaos. We had a great time though, and everyone's creations looked amazing! I continued familiarizing myself with Zoom as I grew my clientele with my coaching program, meeting with women virtually to help them form healthier habits. You would be shocked at what a few little changes over three to six months will do!

As much as I loved experimenting in the kitchen, I realized that, in this digital age, I needed to continue to spread the word about ROOT Mindful Nutrition online. But the idea of social media was alien to me. The hashtags, the reels, the tagging—it was all so overwhelming at first. I was a maestro in the kitchen but a novice in the virtual world. Yet, I knew I had to adapt to keep my passion alive and allow it to reach the masses. It's during times like this that one truly understands the value of connection and community.

My entrepreneur friends in both France and Miami became my guiding lights. From creating my website as a place for people to view my recipes and get in touch for coaching sessions, to setting up my Instagram profile and giving me the basics of filming, they provided me with the training wheels I so desperately needed. I began to post daily about my recipes, tips, and stories.

And as the engagement grew, so did my confidence. My neighbor, who's been a good friend for years, managed to secure a slot for me to contribute a monthly recipe in our community magazine. This incredible support network truly reaffirmed the age-old saying that with a little help from our friends, anything is possible.

As the momentum grew, I kept looking for more opportunities to spread the word about ROOT Mindful Nutrition. It wasn't just about visibility, it was about helping people realize the transformative power of mindful eating. Gradually, people started coming to me with new projects and opportunities. I teamed up with a friend of mine, a tennis coach, and together we created a short film on what to eat before and after a workout. The collaboration was fruitful in so many ways—not only did it draw attention to my brand, but it also solidified my belief in the power of partnerships. When people with different skill sets come together, the results can be truly magical.

To bridge the gap between knowledge and practice, the next step in my journey was designing the RESET Meal Plan eBook. More than just a diet, this is a way for people to jumpstart their health journeys in the comfort of their own homes. The plan includes five consecutive days' worth of recipes, each promising a culinary experience that pampers the palate while nourishing the body. I encourage people to follow a simple format to break down old eating behaviors and make room for healthy new habits: liquid (NutriSmoothie), solid (NutriBowl), and liquid (NutriSoup). Drawing from the richness of plant-based ingredients, each recipe supports hormonal balance, efficient digestion, and an optimized metabolism. And true to my French roots, every dish is a symphony of flavors, textures, and aromas, all while being low in sugar, both gluten and dairy-free and super easy to make! The five-day plan also includes a curated grocery shopping guide and daily at-home workouts to complement the nutrition-focused approach.

I received incredible feedback about the plan from women I didn't even know and wanted to provide an option for those who wanted to take a deeper plunge. So, I created the three-week CLEAN Eating Challenge eBook which promotes the gradual reintroduction of clean animal protein along with nutritious dinner recipes that replace the NutriSoups in the third week, further diversifying the culinary experience. Meanwhile, I also continued to prepare and deliver my RESET Meal Plan and juice cleanses to clients throughout Coral Gables.

ROOT Mindful Nutrition is more than just a brand to me—it's a commitment, a promise to help people develop healthy habits that allow them to feel their best, all without compromising on taste. But it's not just about the food. It's about the stories behind every dish, every ingredient, every bite. It's about making connections with one another, something that's increasingly become a big part of what I do.

One chilly morning in January, an epiphany struck. Why not invite people into my kitchen? That's when the idea of "Meet Me in the Kitchen" cooking classes sprouted. I was stepping into unknown terrain, with a mere three weeks to find a theme, orchestrate content, design an invite, and transform my kitchen into a makeshift studio. The journey, though daunting, was exhilarating, culminating in sessions that were both enlightening and brimming with laughter. I just hosted my latest class, where I gathered six Miami influencers to create nutritious and delicious lunch bowls for busy women, and we had a blast.

Today, I've come to realize that wellness isn't a permanent state—we all face setbacks, but I am now so much more able to overcome them with the toolbox I've gathered over the years, and I find so much fulfillment in helping others do the same. By marrying the essence of culinary artistry with the principles of nutrition and health coaching, I've been able to create an approach that is uniquely mine. This synergy is palpable, with new opportunities, connections, and the expansion of my purpose unveiling themselves every day. As I approach the completion of my executive chef certification at the Mariano Moreno Culinary Institute in Miami, I am filled with excitement about the possibility of elevating my RESET Meal Plans to a whole new level and the opportunities ahead. Soon, I'll be joining Health Chefs as they expand their presence in Miami, where I'll be part of a network of private chefs helping families who want to eat healthy. I can't wait to take on this new chapter and continue my journey!

ROOT Mindful Nutrition has gone farther than I could've ever hoped for, and yet there is still so much more I can create with this brand. Every step of the journey has its lessons, like the time I was on the verge of sealing a deal on a health café in South Miami. When someone outbid me, I took it as a sign and stepped away. Ironically, every day I pass by the café, I see it mostly empty. I realize it might not have been the best fit for me, especially with the responsibilities of raising my three kids. Without that "loss," I would've never chosen the path of a private health chef, which is all I dream of now. From this experience, I learned that if something doesn't happen, it probably wasn't meant for me in the first place.

I often still find myself reminiscing about that little kitchen near Paris, where my love for food was born while watching my mother cook. That same passion has traveled with me across continents, and the lessons I learned from my journey thus far have been priceless. The challenges, as overwhelming as they seemed, only strengthened my resolve and taught me resilience. I learned to keep pushing boundaries, to embrace discomfort, and most importantly, to never give up on my dreams.

For every fearless female entrepreneur out there, let your passion be your compass. Remember that challenges are an integral part of the journey, and with determination, resilience, and a sprinkle of creativity, the world is yours to conquer. Leverage the power of collaboration and community, and know that you don't have to walk your path alone.

Sophie Teixeira

Sophie Teixeira de Abreu is a French Nutri-Chef, certified Integrative Nutrition Health Coach, and entrepreneur based in Miami. She started her career in the luxury cosmetic industry but pivoted towards inner beauty after being diagnosed with subclinical hypothyroidism. As such, Sophie was determined to heal naturally through food and lifestyle changes. Today, Sophie is a graduate of the Institute for Integrative Nutrition (IIN), one of the world's most respected nutrition and health coaching schools. She is also completing her certification as an executive chef at the Mariano Moreno Culinary Institute in Miami. Instead of following the latest fad diet, Sophie promotes a plant-rich, nutrient-dense diet to support hormonal balance, digestion, and metabolism. Flavors, textures, and aromas play a pivotal role in her approach, in alignment with the savoir vivre of her native France. Today, she empowers people to take back their health through her coaching and RESET Meal Plan offering. Additionally, Sophie generously shares her expertise and insights on her platform, ROOT Mindful Nutrition, and is a regular guest on various media outlets including Thrive Magazine, Women's Fitness Magazine, IMPACT Magazine, and Best Holistic Life Magazine, to name a few. Her unwavering passion for promoting healthy cooking and eating has earned her invitations from all over the U.S. and beyond such as the Biohacking Congress, Wickedly Smart Women, Biohacking With Brittany, and many others.

Connect with Sophie at

https://www.root-mindfulnutrition.com/.

CHAPTER 13
When Nothing Is What It Seems

by Sylvia Chavez

Dedicated to every individual who fills my heart with boundless love, and to you, the reader, for graciously welcoming me into your life. You deserve to love deeply and be deeply loved.

Where do I even begin? Today's chapter is a testament to the indomitable spirit that resides within each of us. It's a narrative of triumph over adversity, a journey that unveils the raw and often painful realities of life, yet ultimately celebrates the power we possess to rise above it all.

Since my earliest memories as a little girl, I harbored an unstoppable spirit. In the vast expanse of my imagination, I believed the world was mine to explore freely, with the wings of boundless possibilities at my disposal. Little did I know that life had its own plans and its script to unfold, knitting a tapestry of challenges and resilience.

It's a truth often overlooked that free spirits (especially those embodied by young girls like me) face a world not always ready to embrace their untamed essence. Global statistics reveal a sobering reality – one in three women experiences violence, and according to the National Sexual Violence Resource Center (NSVRC), one in five women in the United States faces completed or attempted rape during their lifetime.

My journey into these stark realities began at the tender age of five, marked by a painful encounter with sexual assault. My free spirit, once soaring high, was grounded in fear, and I felt compelled to create barriers to protect myself from the perceived dangers of the world.

Unfortunately, I was part of the statistics. For many, many years I felt that the world was a dangerous zone and I needed to survive on my own.

For me, struggle, violence, and the chaotic hum of my surroundings became the norm. Behind the facade of a seemingly normal family, my home was a battleground. Constant arguments, my parents' incessant fights, my mother's use of harsh words toward everyone else in the family, and the normalization of physical violence molded an environment where I became a "rebel without a cause," as my Mom used to call me. Little could she understand the multitude of causes that shaped my responses; how could a little girl explain all the reasons she had to respond in that way? It was a far cry from the dream life others believed I was living.

I had unknowingly embraced a survival mode that, over time, became a crooked lens through which I perceived the world. The manifestation of my actions was intricately tied to the survival mode deep-rooted in me during childhood and the necessity to shield myself from the world that surrounded me.

We never had much money at home, but my mom was a total superhero. She managed to do everything. She'd cook homemade meals from scratch, bake bread, sew our fancy party outfits, and keep the house clean; she did it all so smoothly that we hardly noticed we were short on cash.

Mom was like an unstoppable force, and she was my hero and role model when I became a mom.

As the years passed, my inner little rebel was still stuck in that mental danger zone, convinced it needed a fortress to protect her heart and herself from everything and everyone. I constructed a life based on the belief that I was inadequate, damaged, and broken. With such a mindset, how could one possibly foster healthy relationships?

Fast forward to my grand entrance into marriage, and guess what? I chose someone who could perfectly orchestrate a symphony of confirmation for my beliefs. Day one of marital bliss kicked off my residency in Unhappinessville, and for the longest time I pointed fingers at him. It was ignorance, indeed. How could I know better?

Today, I've held the profound truth that we are the architects of our universes. If you step into a partnership with the notion that you're not worthy of something better, chances are you'll end up with someone who won't appreciate you and might even ignore you. Your beliefs shape your reality, and I, my friend, was a walking testament to that.

I spent nearly two decades in a place that felt more like a loveless void, where care was as scarce as rain in the desert.

There exists two approaches to undertaking the same task: a healthy one and an unhealthy one. Mine? Well, it leaned toward the not-so-healthy side. My heart and soul were pretty beat up, and everything I did back then was more of a gut reaction than a thoughtful action. I was walking around thinking I was fine, but deep down, I was getting emptier by the day.

My free spirit left me for a long time but one magic day it decided to show up in a big way!

There was this constant voice inside me – a faint whisper at first, gradually building up to an urgent scream, pushing me to take charge of my life. I felt trapped, disheartened, and drained of vitality, prompting me to reach a pivotal moment. It was crystal clear when I told myself, "Enough is enough" – the resonance of my voice hitting me like never before. I could not stand one more minute living in survival mode. I was dying inside, sick and tired of feeling miserable and blaming everyone else but myself. I left that life to start a new one, with no guarantees but with HOPE.

A fresh opportunity lay before me. It's hard to count the times I yearned to rise again or the occasions I messed up royally. Ignorance was my companion; there were things I didn't know, and I found myself in need of learning how to live all over again.

I came across this saying that goes, "When the disciple is ready, the master will appear." And that exactly happened to me. I was ready to be challenged to my core and that's when my journey toward loving myself truly began.

I'm all about saying yes to things that are legal and safe, so anything related to personal growth gets a spot on my calendar. I dove into learning from various masters – Enneagram, Breathwork, Counseling, Coaching, Astrology, Gestalt, Akashic Records, and more. I even embarked on a sacred four-day journey to Machu Picchu, where a shaman worked his magic on me. For the first time in my life, I felt like I was finally on the road to discovering and loving myself. Picture it like a beautiful sunrise in my life – I could finally see the light at the end of the tunnel.

During this part of my journey, I went through a pretty ugly divorce and I moved to a house of my own with my four kids. During the process of getting the divorce finalized, I had no money at all so I started looking for ways to "survive" again. This was a different kind of survival, I felt free and filled with the strength that this freedom gave me. Remember? I was unstoppable and I knew to take one day at a time and reach out for help. I believed in myself, and all the work that I had done up until then with all the teachers, courses, masters, and coaches finally paid off.

I firmly believe there is a reason for everything in life. I was confident that, regardless of the challenges surrounding me, I would uncover a solution. It wasn't easy, my friend. There were days filled with uncertainty, moments of shedding tears, lots of desperation, and a sprinkle of inspiring days. They say people either thrive out of desperation or inspiration and let me tell you, that's true!

I employed every tool I knew during those challenging times. I turned to prayer with all my heart – reaching out to God, my guardian angel, my ancestors, and every higher power I could summon. Let me assure you, my prayers did not fall on deaf ears!

So, if you find yourself in a place like where I once stood, pray with all your heart, extend your reach, seek help, and persist in your quest. Even in the bleakest moments, there's a glimmer of light somewhere.

I worked to pay for my studies so I could finish my career in Counseling specializing in Personal Development. The great part of studying is that I could use every tool to heal myself and grow.

Achieving mastery in life begins when you take responsibility for every aspect of it. It's undeniably a challenging lesson, demanding moments of pain and transformation, but the journey is entirely worthwhile. Once you grasp that your life is your creation, for better or worse, you gain the ability to architect it intentionally.

No longer cast as a victim of circumstances beyond your control, you start viewing challenges as significant opportunities for growth, increased happiness, and a heightened sense of vitality. It's like upgrading your life by design, my friend.

I dedicated myself to healing my inner child, addressing my past, working through traumas, and nurturing my body daily. Healing is an ongoing process that may span a lifetime, but within that journey, each day unfolds as an infinite opportunity to love and find happiness.

And then, one extraordinary day, I met the love of my life. I was in a space to draw in the right person – someone who resonated with the love I had cultivated for myself, to the extent that I refused to settle for anything less than everything.

And again, I proved to myself that life is magical, beautiful, and worth "living." Our story was a love story from the very beginning. Beyond all the differences among the two of us, there was something much bigger that drew us together.

He was single, never married, had no kids, and was five years younger than me. In contrast, I was divorced, older, had four kids, and held a strong belief that if a man was still single at 38, there might be something off.

Beliefs, oh beliefs! What do you believe in, especially when it comes to relationships? Those beliefs can be the shackles that hold you back in the past, maybe even still today. I'm throwing out an invitation to reconsider them and swap them out for new beliefs that work in your favor, making you happier, healthier, and feeling more loved.

Now, back to my tale – we fell head over heels and continued building our family together. He made the move into my house, joining my four kids – Paz, Sol, Facu, and Fer (8, 9, 17, and 21 years old, respectively) – not to forget my trusty dog, Nicolas.

He turned out to be the missing piece of the puzzle, showering us with joy and love. We tied the knot and constructed a home filled with love, appreciation, and a whole lot of communication.

But wait, there's more – our joy expanded even further with the arrival of another bundle of joy. Sofia came into our lives through in-vitro, and I welcomed her at the age of 44, though I spent most of the pregnancy in bed.

During those months, my husband Alejandro took charge of everything. From getting the kids to school, hitting the supermarket, and keeping the house spick and span, to cooking up a storm – he was the ultimate chauffeur for the kids. Plus, he tended to me and the baby every single day, always with a beaming smile on his face.

This was new territory for me. I was accustomed to doing everything solo, without much support, and suddenly I found myself in a world where I was pampered, loved, adored, and cared for. When Sofia woke up in the middle of the night, he was there, taking care of her so I could catch some sleep. He relished every moment with our baby, even if it meant sacrificing some shut-eye. He did it all with an abundance of love, and he continues to do so, even after 20 years.

Picture this: one day, we had friends popping over for dinner, and I was running late from my office. I needed to grab groceries, do the prep, and get myself ready. While on my way home, I called him to give a heads-up about my situation. Brace yourself for his unexpected response: "No worries. I've got everything covered. You don't have to lift a finger, love. Just come over and take some time to relax before our friends arrive." I was behind the wheel, and I vividly remember having to pull over because I burst into tears. I couldn't believe it – I felt an overwhelming sense of gratitude and love. And let me tell you, even then and certainly now, I don't take this incredible man for granted. No matter what he does, I make it a point to say thank you, reminding myself to appreciate him. That, my friend, is love. I love him more today than yesterday and less than tomorrow – our love hasn't waned; it's grown stronger, bolder, and more passionate with each passing day.

He's my rock, my best friend, an amazing father to all my kids, and unquestionably my favorite person in the whole world. It's a blessing. If by chance your current relationship doesn't quite match this vibe, let my story inspire you to build it. There's time! Right now is the perfect moment to start crafting your dream into reality. You deserve it, and settling for anything less is simply not an option!

And here I stand, at the end of a long and incredible adventure up to this very day. Having the right partner can inject so much more interest and fun into your life! And laughter, well, that's a major perk in a good relationship – we've got that, too.

Here's a nugget of wisdom I've picked up along the way: regardless of the circumstances, we're here to break free from cycles – be it violence, scarcity, poverty, unhappiness, or abuse. The barriers that hinder us? They're not real; they exist only in our imagination. We're powerful beings, and if we can dream it, we can create it.

I'm going to level with you – there were times on my journey when I felt like I couldn't make it. Those lofty dreams I had about changing the world seemed like they'd never come to fruition, no matter how hard I pushed. It led me to forget about myself, my body, and what truly mattered. I was so fixated on "doing" that I lost sight of "being." Have you ever found yourself caught in the hamster wheel of achievement, neglecting yourself in the process?

My body served as the ultimate whistleblower! I fell ill, gained lots of weight, and struggled with brain fog, among various other symptoms. Once again, I found myself on a quest for more healing. So, I sought out another teacher, and finally, I was able to heal myself by confronting those neglected areas of my body where the trauma still remained. I relearned the art of breathing, being present in my beautiful and unique body, and consciously taking each breath. Love, as always, found its way!

Now, here's a truth that might sound simple but holds immense power – we need to breathe! To be truly present in our lives, we must be present in our breathing. If you scrutinize your thoughts closely, you'll likely discover that you spend most of your time elsewhere – thinking about unfinished projects, the kids, the job, the next vacation, money, or someone else but you. This is when your body starts whispering. If you don't pay attention, it eventually resorts to screaming for help –

a painful ordeal. How do I know? Well, you probably already know the answer.

Connecting with my body opened up an additional layer of happiness and fulfillment. I felt unstoppable once more as if I had it all – me, myself, and I! Alongside my power partner and beautiful family, life was complete. Embracing who you are and staying present brings boundless growth opportunities. You must redefine yourself based on infinite possibilities rather than limits.

The journey is ongoing. I was in the process of learning self-care by fostering a connection with my body – the final holistic step towards becoming one, a whole.

Learning to appreciate my successes, both the small victories and the monumental ones, marked a turning point in my life. I established my coaching practice in San Diego, co-authored numerous books, and clinched the title of a 2 times International Bestselling Author – all in the same year. These achievements have enabled me to influence hundreds of women worldwide, guiding them to discover true love by falling passionately in love with themselves.

Reflecting on my journey, I've accomplished more up to this point than many people do in their entire lifetime, and I can't help but feel an overwhelming sense of pride. I now carry a serene assurance that if I were to depart today, I could do so peacefully, knowing I made a difference. I touched countless lives with my love and open heart, and I don't seek external validation because I witness it every day in the eyes that shine again, the hearts that reopen, and the transformative power of love on my clients.

Even this chapter, sharing my story with you, is dedicated to you – the reader – and your boundless potential to conquer everything you've ever dreamed about. It's all about you, the limitless freedom surrounding you and within you. It's about your immense capacity to love, be loved, and cherish yourself like never before.

I sincerely hope my story has sparked inspiration within you to craft your own narrative – a tale of happiness, fulfillment, and joy. Picture a love story surpassing your wildest dreams, narrating a journey of success and impactful contributions to the world.

And as for me, well, I'm just getting started again – remember? I am unstoppable! And guess what? So are you.

Sylvia Chavez

Meet Sylvia Chavez, renowned as America's Love Queen, an International Speaker, a two-time International Bestselling Author, Show Host, and Love and Relationship Mentor, boasting over 19 years of experience positively impacting the lives of countless women worldwide in their pursuit of true love.

Sylvia, also known as "The Love Expert," has successfully deciphered the intricate RELATIONSHIP CODE, consistently applying it in her marriage for the past 20 years. A happy mother of five children, aged 17 to 39, and a grandmother, she cherishes precious moments with her husband and loved ones. Additionally, Sylvia is a talented singer who shares her passion with her husband, Alejandro, an extraordinary saxophonist and singer.

Beyond her roles, Sylvia is an intuitive and wise woman, adept at understanding the emotions and needs of others. She can guide individuals to unexplored facets of themselves, encouraging them to embrace their greatness and attract the love they desire in life.

Are you prepared to script a love story that surpasses your wildest dreams, refusing to settle for anything less than the true desires of your soul and heart?

Connect with Sylvia at https://linktr.ee/sylviachavez.

Dear Reader,

As you turn this final page, you might find yourself reflecting on the journey you've just experienced through these words. Each story you read is a tapestry of dreams, struggles, triumphs, and the relentless spirit of its creator. Now, imagine a world where your story joins these ranks – where your voice, your experiences, and your unique perspective are shared and celebrated.

This is not just an invitation; it's a call to action from Action Takers Publishing. We believe in the power of stories to transform, inspire, and connect humankind. More importantly, we believe in your story and its potential to make a significant impact on the world.

Why wait for "someday" to tell your story? The time is now, and the world is ready to listen. Whether it's a tale of adventure, a deeply personal memoir, a groundbreaking idea, or a story that has been quietly growing in your heart, it deserves to be told.

At Action Takers Publishing, led by our Founder & CEO, Lynda Sunshine, we specialize in turning visions into reality. We understand the journey of transforming a personal narrative into a published book – it's a journey of courage, creativity, and breaking through fears. Our team is dedicated to guiding you through every step of this exhilarating process, from the initial draft to the moment your book is held in the hands of eager readers across the globe.

Join our vibrant community of authors, a diverse group of storytellers who have dared to make their voices heard. With us, you'll find more than just a publisher; you'll discover a supportive network of mentors, editors, and fellow authors who are all committed to the success of your story.

Take the leap. Embrace the thrill of seeing your name on the cover of your very own book. Contact us at Action Takers Publishing, and let's embark on this remarkable journey together. Your story matters, and the time to share it with the world is now.

Nothing Happens Without Action.
Lynda Sunshine West
Founder & CEO
Action Takers Publishing
www.ActionTakersPublishing.com

P.S. Remember, every great story begins with a simple decision to start writing. Yours is no different. Let's make it happen, together.

READER BONUS!

Dear Reader,

As a thank you for your support, Action Takers Publishing would like to offer you a special reader bonus: a free download of our course, "How to Write, Publish, Market & Monetize Your Book the Fast, Fun & Easy Way." This comprehensive course is designed to provide you with the tools and knowledge you need to bring your book to life and turn it into a successful venture.

The course typically **retails for $499**, but as a valued reader, you can access it for free. To claim your free download, simply follow this link ActionTakersPublishing.com/workshops - use the discount code "coursefree" to get a 100% discount and start writing your book today.

If we are still giving away this course by the time you're reading this book, head straight over to your computer and start the course now. It's absolutely free.

READER BONUS!

ActionTakersPublishing.com/workshops
discount code "coursefree"

Printed in Great Britain
by Amazon